FOLLOW THE WATER

FOLLOW  THE WATER

The Unbelievable True Story of
a Teenager's Survival in the Amazon

ELLEN COCHRANE
Illustrated by Caroline Church

LITTLE, BROWN AND COMPANY
New York   Boston

Text copyright © 2026 by Ellen Cochrane
Illustrations copyright © 2026 by Caroline Church

Twisted vines © Incomible/Shutterstock.com
Plane © Kalinsky/Shutterstock.com
Leaf icon © Oleksandr Poliashenko/Shutterstock.com

Cover art copyright © 2026 by Mike Heath. Cover design by Gabrielle Chang.
Cover copyright © 2026 by Hachette Book Group, Inc.
Interior design by Carla Weise.

Hachette Book Group supports the right to free expression and the value of copyright. The purpose of copyright is to encourage writers and artists to produce the creative works that enrich our culture.

The scanning, uploading, and distribution of this book without permission is a theft of the author's intellectual property. If you would like permission to use material from the book (other than for review purposes), please contact permissions@hbgusa.com. Thank you for your support of the author's rights.

Little, Brown and Company
Hachette Book Group
1290 Avenue of the Americas, New York, NY 10104
LBYR.com

First Edition: March 2026

Little, Brown and Company is a division of Hachette Book Group, Inc. The Little, Brown name and logo are registered trademarks of Hachette Book Group, Inc.

The publisher is not responsible for websites (or their content) that are not owned by the publisher.

Little, Brown and Company books may be purchased in bulk for business, educational, or promotional use. For information, please contact your local bookseller or the Hachette Book Group Special Markets Department at special.markets@hbgusa.com.

Library of Congress Cataloging-in-Publication Data
Names: Cochrane, Ellen (Ellen M.) author | Church, Caroline illustrator
Title: Follow the water : the unbelievable true story of a teenager's survival in the Amazon / Ellen Cochrane ; illustrated by Caroline Church.
Description: First edition. | New York : Little, Brown and Company, 2026. | Includes bibliographical references. | Audience: Ages 10–14 | Summary: "The true story of a girl who fell out of a plane over the Amazon and walked out of the jungle eleven days later." —Provided by publisher.
Identifiers: LCCN 2025016021 | ISBN 9781523528639 hardcover | ISBN 9781523528653 ebook
Subjects: LCSH: Koepcke, Juliane—Juvenile literature | Airplane crash survival—Peru—Juvenile literature | Aircraft accident victims—Peru—Biography—Juvenile literature | Jungle survival—Amazon River Region—Juvenile literature | Naturalists—Germany—Biography—Juvenile literature | LCGFT: Literature. | Biographies.
Classification: LCC TL553.9 .C63 2026 | DDC 363.12/4092 $a B—dc23/eng/20250606
LC record available at https://lccn.loc.gov/2025016021

ISBNs: 978-1-5235-2863-9 (hardcover), 978-1-5235-2865-3 (ebook)

Printed in Indiana, USA

LSC-C

Printing 1, 2025

For Pat

CONTENTS

PROLOGUE
The Vow..1

CHAPTER ONE
Childhood 5

CHAPTER TWO
Christmas Eve..23

CHAPTER THREE
Christmas Morning...38

CHAPTER FOUR
The Search 54

CHAPTER FIVE
Follow the Water 60

CHAPTER SIX
The Daily Struggle 71

CHAPTER SEVEN
The Boat..88

CHAPTER EIGHT
At Last..105

CHAPTER NINE
A Different Kind of Storm...116

CHAPTER TEN
A Return Home 126

CHAPTER ELEVEN
Germany..132

CHAPTER TWELVE
Herzog 135

CHAPTER THIRTEEN
Another Journey 141

EPILOGUE 147

ACKNOWLEDGMENTS 155
BEYOND THE CANOPY 157
HOW TO BECOME A SCIENTIST... 167
FURTHER READING AND VIEWING.................................. 173
BIBLIOGRAPHY.. 175

PROLOGUE
THE VOW

A slim girl huddles *on an Amazon riverbank. She wills herself not to scratch the hundreds of bites swelling on her skin. Insect hums and the whispers of wings fill her ears. The thick cocoa-brown water grows black in the deepening night. Clumps of logs and spiky palm fronds drift silently past her. Shadows of deciduous trees and dangling liana vines loom overhead.*

The nocturnal noises begin. She hears snorts, pants, the treads of hooves and padding paws. She is stranded. There are no roads, no boats, and no phones. Her watch stopped ticking days ago. She wears one sandal and a minidress. Her only tools are her brain and her body. The nearest human hearts beat far away, many miles downriver. People are too far to hear her, too far to even imagine a girl alone in the endless jungle.

FOLLOW THE WATER

No one would blame the girl if she gave up. Who would scold her if she decided to wait for help, rolled herself into a tight fetal position, and closed her eyes to dream forever on the riverbank sand?

The safety of dreams would give her conversations with her parents and her mother's strong but delicate hand to hold. Her father would beat her at chess, and she would be dry, warm, and cozy. In her dreams she could snuggle with her German shepherd, Lobo. Her skin would stop throbbing, and the screaming, relentless itchiness would fade away. In her dreams the plane would land safely. She would not be injured and entirely alone in the Amazon jungle for days, miles from her home, family, and other people—fighting for her life.

A single, heavy raindrop plops into the river. Rings ripple outward from the spot it enters. Two more follow, then ten, then thousands of raindrops tumble out of the sky. The surface of the river is laced with connecting water rings. Raindrops land on her hair and neck and soak her flower-print dress. Rain sounds wrap around her like a curtain. The repetitive plinks consume the silence. Water on water. Water rolling off oval leaves with pointy tips and careening along the spines of sharp palm fronds. Water plopping on stones and branches. Water sinking into sand. She lifts her chin, and water strikes her swollen, bruised eyes and then trickles down her face. Thin streaks of mud mix with tears and rainwater and line her cheeks.

The insects find shelter. Frogs sing in a discordant chant to the rhythm of the falling rain. They creep and hop in the

THE VOW

night gloom. The scents of decaying plant matter, soil, unseen river creatures, and hints of wood bark crowd into the air.

The future tumbles away from her. The memories of her life at home are clear but distant. Her mind is focused.

She understands her predicament. She is in trouble. She could die here.

An aching loss for her mother seeps through her body. She knows her mother is here too, lost, but hasn't seen her since the accident. Despair swells in her heart, travels up her throat, and then settles in her head. Her emotions shift to thought. I will find my mother. I will get home. *She reins in feelings, as strong as a hurtling train, and makes a vow.*

I must be alive for a reason. My life must mean something. If I survive, I will make a difference in the world.

CHAPTER ONE
CHILDHOOD

A shrill whistle cuts through the rainforest canopy. Juliane Koepcke and her mother, Maria, stand on the riverbank of the Yuyapichis River, watching for Hans Koepcke. They wear dirt-splattered clothes, headscarves, and rubber swamp boots and carry machetes.

Soon Hans's lithe figure and Lobo, a jubilant German shepherd, appear on the opposite shore. The whistle was Hans's cue to pole the longboat across the water to pick up his wife and daughter. It is the dog's signal to spin and bark with excitement.

It took three days for Maria and Juliane to travel 450 miles to reach home. After a short flight over the sawtooth peaks of the Andes Mountains, they bumped along in a mud-plastered four-wheeler that rumbled over unfinished roads, occasionally stopping so they could hack through vines and scrub, to reach a remote jungle outpost. But their journey was far from over. When those roads gave out, they continued by boat, winding for hours along thick green channels of the river, pushing even deeper into the heart of the Amazon. Overnight stops were spent at small settlements along the shores. They disembarked from the last boat ride still many miles from their destination. Mother and daughter, now on foot, used machetes to hack through dense stretches of overgrown jungle, following trails that at times disappeared into the forest. As they trudged on, flies, mosquitoes, and midges made beelines for any exposed skin.

Juliane is fourteen. She has no brothers or sisters and left behind all the comforts of city life. She misses her friends, milkshakes, and her school. She misses her bed. Initially, the idea of abandoning the comforts, school, and social life of Lima irked her. And heading off into the wilds to live with just her parents was not thrilling. But the richly blooming red flowers, mango trees, citrus fruits, and the luxurious deep green of the jungle erase her doubts. The isolated world of the Amazon wilderness is rich with life and beauty.

She soon shares her parents' joy at finding this perfect spot near the cloud forest of the El Sira mountain range. Here on the gently rolling hills, by the lip of the

CHILDHOOD

river, they will build a scientific research station. Juliane surveys her new world from the riverbank and watches her father guide the boat closer. She is ready for the isolation and sacrifices that will come. *After all, I am the child of scientists*, she thinks.

Long before Juliane was born, Hans and Maria met as biology students at a university in Germany and quickly became engaged. After struggling to find jobs as scientists in the devastated post–World War II German economy, Hans received an offer to work as a zoologist for the Javier Prado Museum of Natural History in Lima, Peru. It was 1948. He promised to pave the way for them both and left with little more than a letter of introduction in his pocket, verifying his university degrees and a promised job in Lima, Peru.

But after the war, German citizens could not travel freely, and Hans did not have permission to leave the country. Undaunted, he slipped under a border fence into Austria and then trekked his way through Italy, France, and Spain as an undocumented immigrant. He stowed away on a ship in Spain and finally crossed the Atlantic Ocean to reach Brazil.

Hans was now in South America, but on the wrong side of the continent. Three thousand miles stood between him and Lima, Peru. His journey began on foot on the rudimentary roads of the Brazilian Pantanal, a huge wetland region, and then into the Amazon forest. He managed to take a plane over the Andes Mountains to reach Lima. Two years after leaving Germany, the sun-browned, sinewy, weatherworn scientist presented himself to the startled administration at the university to secure a job at the Javier Prado Museum of Natural History.

That same year, Maria completed her studies and successfully obtained permission to join him. She made her journey without difficulty, and the couple married not long after she arrived in Lima. They began dual careers as university instructors and research scientists working for the natural history museum.

By the time Juliane was born in 1954, Hans and Maria were traveling and researching the twenty-four departments (the equivalents of states) of Peru. Both parents were overjoyed with the family addition, and as soon as she could walk, Juliane accompanied them on the research trips, only staying at home during the most dangerous journeys.

Even though they both taught at the university, they really belonged outdoors observing birds and animals, collecting specimens, and writing notes. Nothing escaped their scrutiny. Maria's artistic talents were widely admired, and she was commissioned to create airmail stamps depicting birds of Peru.

The pair worked so closely together it was impossible

CHILDHOOD

to talk about one without mentioning the other. Where Maria was gregarious and outgoing, Hans was a formal person with few close friends. Both had an intense nature and a hunger for learning and teaching. They were the perfect team: married to each other, to the type of lives they wanted to live, and to science.

Maria and Hans published scientific papers and collaborated on many of them. Hans undertook a systematic ecological survey and inventory of species in Panguana, while Maria published *The Birds of the Department of Lima, Peru,* illustrated with her pen-and-ink drawings. Her book was intended as a commercial field guide for ornithologists as well as for the student or hobbyist. Maria planned on completing natural history bird books for each department in the country.

Juliane soon went to the museum with her parents. She pattered along the checkerboard floor tiles of the cavernous halls. Her piping voice and laughter echoed through the displays of Peruvian animals, plants, and dinosaur fossils. Although she sometimes feared the mummy display, the cool halls soon became a second home. Before long she joined her parents on explorations of the Peruvian wilderness. The daily dangers and struggles on these trips tested the small girl's fortitude.

Young Juliane had blonde-white hair and a pixie

FOLLOW THE WATER

face. In the wilderness she wore khaki pants, cotton shirts, and a kerchief on her head and carried a miniature backpack. She and her parents gathered wood for fuel and warmed themselves around cook fires. They snuggled up together at night.

When her mother led her across rocky Andes trails, Juliane followed with confidence. Her father's tall, straight back was her guidepost as she stepped high through jungle paths, avoiding the brambles and, at times, life-threatening danger that lurked there. Both parents never passed an opportunity to share information to keep her safe. "Look, Juliane. There's a bushmaster—one of the most poisonous snakes in the world," her mother warned. "They're very aggressive. You must be on your guard against them."

BUSHMASTER SNAKES
The bushmaster—the longest venomous snake found in the Amazon—kills more than half the people who suffer its bite. Many victims never even see the snake that attacks them.

The snake is a member of the pit viper family, which includes rattlesnakes. It has a deep pit between its eyes and nostrils on each side of its head. The pit is the opening to the source of a sixth sense: a pair of hypersensitive, infrared-detecting organs that give the snake the ability to sense heat and judge the size and location of warm-blooded prey, even in the dead of night.

This limbless reptile nestles into leaves and crevices on the moist forest floor and waits patiently for its next meal. Diamond-shaped patterns on its mostly brown body camouflage it perfectly.

The unlucky human who walks into its strike zone can receive a swift, accurate bite. When the venom attacks the human body, symptoms of nausea, vomiting, shock, and heart malfunction occur. A powerful antivenom is needed to reverse the effects.

Female bushmasters lay five to nineteen eggs in a clutch. The mother builds a burrow to protect her brood until the eggs hatch and will lash out fiercely at anything that comes close to her nest. The hatchlings have fully developed venom and fangs. They are left to fend for themselves once they break through their shells. Adults can grow up to ten feet long and weigh as much as eleven pounds.

At first, Juliane only watched her parents weigh birds, measure feathers, and note behaviors. Soon she helped collect leaf specimens and observe animal activity. Her mother made notes and sketched plants, mammals, birds, and geological features. Her father wrote detailed accounts of all the living creatures he encountered. Local people and Indigenous tribes were amazed by the tiny child who stepped and climbed so confidently in the wilderness. After their initial surprise, they guided the three Koepckes into the deepest parts of the wilderness.

Her parents patiently challenged her to adapt, and despite the hardships Juliane reveled in the journeys. What might make a city child scared or uncomfortable was second nature to her. The family rarely slept in soft beds and ate over a camp cookstove. Frost and rainstorms drove them deep under the covers at night. She slept anywhere. She tucked in under blankets in a truck bed stalled in the Andes due to mudslide danger. The sandy banks of Amazon River tributaries were her mattresses and the mat of vegetation of the rainforest her walls. Sleeping bags on deserted Pacific Ocean beaches protected her from the night chill. In the Andes she washed up in glacial lakes. She rested beneath mosquito nets in the cloud forests, and in the Atacama Desert she drifted away to billions of twinkling stars overhead. During the day, humidity, altitude, and high temperatures slowed their bodies down. Yet Juliane never complained and became a miniature helper for her parents in the face of all these challenges.

Juliane learned from every encounter with the wild. She rode in truck beds through rocky mountain bluffs so high that today's travelers carry oxygen tanks to avoid severe altitude sickness. She clung to the sides

CHILDHOOD

of the vehicles as they crossed rickety log bridges on four-wheelers.

Her parents encouraged her to shake off minor physical and mental discomfort. They warmed her up when she got too cold and always made sure she was watched and safe. Each location brought new lessons. "Nightjars live here," said her mother as they peered into a cave near the jungle town of Tingo María. "These birds can find their way with echolocation, and their body fat can be used to light oil lamps. People also call them oilbirds."

On the water she knew to sit still in boats and not stand or move without thinking. Before she was a teen, she learned to slide canoes noiselessly away from the riverbanks using twelve-foot poles to steer. In rough waters the family rode with master boatmen who navigated the pull of the river currents. They showed the family which river bends to choose and how to approach churning eddies and rapids. "If you get lost in the jungle and you find flowing water, then stay near it, follow its course. It will bring you to other people," her father said. Cool breezes and water sprayed over her face in these boats. She traveled the rivers with no terror of the towering green jungle walls that framed the riverbanks.

During the school year she lived in Humboldt House, the Koepckes' sprawling home in Lima. Here Juliane shared her home with live owls, snakes, parrots, and collections of bizarre and rare Amazon insects. She would join her parents at dinner with a revolving cast of research scientists. Her parents' colleagues stayed at Juliane's house before they launched expeditions into the rainforest or mountains, and they rested there on their return. Clumps of backpacks, mud-encrusted boots, and trunks lay in the guest rooms. Men with grizzled beards and women with tousled heads of hair sat around the dinner table. It was the focal point for ornithologists and other scientists doing fieldwork in Peru.

Her parents and their friends drank endless cups of strong tea and devoured fluffy German pastries. Flushed faces and excited conversations in German and Spanish revealed the scientists' passion. Their love and admiration of the wild Amazon and amazement at new discoveries gushed into Juliane's ears. It was sometimes late at night when she finally went to bed, the intensity of the evenings still bouncing through her head.

The scientists and her parents brought living and dead specimens home, turning the house into a laboratory. Once, Hans and Maria discovered a large species of shark at the local market. They bought it and plopped it on the dining table for dissection. When her father carefully drew the scalpel across the abdomen and sliced open the stomach, a human hand tumbled out. The victim was most likely an escapee from a notorious island prison off the coast of Lima. The hand went to the police, and the shark went on exhibit at the natural history museum.

CHILDHOOD

Then, in 1968, when Juliane was fourteen, her parents' research dream came true. The government gave them permission to purchase land to create a scientific research station in the Amazon. The Koepckes wanted an ideal spot to study birds, animals, and the ecosystem. They searched for the perfect area in the lowland Amazon forest framed on one side by the western foothills of the El Sira mountain range.

The family needed to establish their home and research station in a location where they could live year-round. During the summer rainy season, snowmelt from the Andes dissolves into a watershed that flows eastward, forming small streams and rivers. More than one hundred inches of yearly rainfall adds to the melting snow. Thousands of rivers form, swell, and rip through the forest. Small trickles join streams, and streams join powerful rivers. The rainy season storms could easily flood out a poorly chosen spot.

In a stroke of great luck, the family befriended Carlos Aquiles Vásquez de Módena, known as Moro by his friends. He lived and farmed in the Yuyapichis River region and helped the Koepckes locate the ideal spot and then set up the research station. He transported the family's gear and developed relationships with the area's residents. In coming years, he would be instrumental in the upkeep and running of the station.

They named the station Panguana. This was the

local name for a small brown-eyed bird of the forest. Juliane left school in Lima and moved permanently to the forest with her parents. Her home address was now 450 miles from Lima, a speck on the map amid the largest rainforest jungle on Earth. She became a true jungle child.

The family's new home was part of an abandoned Indigenous village. They chose a home rested on stilts to avoid floods. It had a palm leaf roof thatched with liana vines and was level with the tree canopy. Juliane's first bed was a sleeping bag and mat on the hard wooden floor in a small room next to her parents. All cooking was done over outdoor wood fires. Rice, beans, harvested fruits, brocket deer, and local roots were on the menu. They struggled to keep the wood dry enough to easily start a fire—humidity and rain challenged the fire starters. Candles and flashlights provided their only light at night.

For baths, Juliane headed to the river. She battled an onslaught of flies and mosquitoes that hovered over the water during each wash. In the following months, real beds, pillows, and mosquito nets slowly made the journey to Panguana. Generators and scientific equipment followed to aid the research. Additional buildings and a bathing hut were built. The research station became a comfortable home.

CHILDHOOD

Juliane's spark of curiosity flamed. Mother and Father were expert teachers, and her favorite schoolroom was the forest. Indeed, her backyard *was* the forest. Birds and insects flew freely through the house. Vampire bats lived in the roof rafters. Howler monkeys bellowed and scampered across the tree branches at eye level. Insects clicked and buzzed nonstop. Stars, spared from the blast of city lights, crowned the sky in twinkling brilliance. Ghostly jungle moons gleamed over the dark twine of vines.

Juliane explored the nearby jungle. She practiced finding her way in the forest alone and wielded her machete like a *machetero*, a forest woodcutter. Her machete notched trees with trail markers. Her eyes read paw prints, broken branches, and snatches of fur or feathers caught on bushes. Deep breaths registered the perfume of rainforest flowers and the inescapable scent of decay.

An already-present empathy with animals deepened. She ran bird hospitals, nursed sick and injured animals, and raised hatched chicks. The Asháninka, an Indigenous people who lived deep in the forest, emerged one day to give her baby parrots. The birds were too young to feed themselves. She chewed up bananas and dropped the mush from her fingertips into their hungry mouths.

ASHÁNINKA

Like most Indigenous Amazonian people, the Asháninka are closely tied to the land. Traditional culture included migration to prime spots for fruit and vegetable farming. They also hunted animals in the rainforest for meat. Today, most Asháninka have settled in permanent farming communities.

Contact with Europeans and the modern world brought problems to the more than fifty native Peruvian Amazon tribes. Early explorers brought disease and violence to the land. Modern timber and mineral merchants threaten destruction of the rainforest.

In the 1990s, Peru changed its constitution, declaring it the government's duty to protect the ethnic and cultural diversity of the nation and to support the rights of Indigenous people. However, Indigenous Peruvians struggle with societal acceptance of their languages and cultures and the abuse of natural resources and pollution.

Anthropologists believe that even today there are tribes deep in the Peruvian rainforest that have little, if any, contact with other people. These people purposefully chose to avoid the majority culture and ventured deep into the jungle, retreating from major rivers and settlements. They are isolated from the twenty-first century and continue to live a lifestyle forged by more than twelve thousand years in the rainforest.

If Juliane had been a traditional Asháninka girl in the 1970s, she would have lived with her extended family in a tidy rainforest compound. Her house would have been of the same type as that in which Juliane lived with her mother and father. The Asháninka were neighbors and frequently visited Juliane and her parents.

Hans ensured that Juliane knew the dangers surrounding her in the forest. In his serious and sometimes gruff manner, he showed her how to start a fire without matches and how to orient herself in the forest without a compass. He explained animal aggression around the protection of the young, and predictable behaviors around food and nests. He instructed Juliane to never put her boots on without shaking them for poisonous spiders and to check her bedding before sleeping.

While Juliane was close to both of her parents, she was especially bonded to her mother. Like Maria, she enjoyed drawing, and they shared a cheerful attitude and excitement about natural history.

On school days, they walked into the jungle at sunrise. The first lesson taught her about scientific methods and the sacrifices scientists needed to make. But it wasn't always pleasant. A cloud of rainforest mosquitoes gathered around them and settled in for a meal. "You must not move now, even if you get bitten." Her mother quietly spoke the instruction and Juliane stopped swatting at them.

FOLLOW THE WATER

Her mother pointed out a sunbittern. She knew the bird would startle if they moved. As they stood still and silent, the unassuming brownish bird stretched its wings wide to display large eyeball-shaped yellow-and-black plumage on each wing. The flash of the orbs made the small bird look like a formidable beast with substantial bulging eyes. "If you want to be a biologist, you have to learn to sacrifice," her mother added in barely a whisper. The pair then stood silent and unmoving. They observed the bird for a quarter of an hour and then seamlessly moved on in the rainforest. They were covered with bites.

These real-life lessons outpaced what she could learn in a city classroom, and Juliane absorbed the complexities and hardships of the rainforest with deftness. Endlessly soggy clothes, bug bites, poisonous plants and animals, showers of rain, and the struggle to secure clean food and drinking water were just part of her daily routine. But she flourished in the environment of learning and discovery. Each morning, Juliane woke to the vibrant, earthy scent of the jungle, accompanied by the melodies and calls of birds in the canopy. Cooling rainstorms offered respite from the equatorial sun, while birds and small mammals became frequent visitors, eventually turning into beloved pets. The unfolding cycles of the natural world around her gave Juliane a rare, intimate view of life in the Amazon.

CHILDHOOD

She was a child of science and the forest, but her parents continued her formal studies, mailed from her school in Lima. She kept up on Spanish, math, and history. In the field, the jungle's green palette became familiar, and plants and trees now stood out as individual species, with common and Latin names, not just a mat of vegetation. Soon she and her mother were eagerly discussing Juliane's future as a biologist.

When the Peruvian authorities learned about Juliane's life in the forest, they insisted she return to Lima to finish her last year of high school. Her parents were required to comply, as they had established the research station in agreement with the government.

It was a bittersweet order. While her parents remained at Panguana in the rainforest, Juliane reunited with classmates and enjoyed the pleasures of the city. But she missed her parents and her jungle home. Every school break and holiday, Juliane traveled a little over an hour by plane over the Andes Mountains, rode a four-wheeler to cross soggy jungle roads, used a pole to navigate rivers, and finally hiked in rubber boots to her home, Panguana.

On December 24 of her senior year, in 1971, she was especially excited about the trip home. Her mother had come to Lima to watch her graduate from high school and was flying back with her. Juliane was now seventeen years old, and after a few months back in the jungle, she would return to Lima to prepare for the *Arbitur*, the entrance exams for universities in Germany. Her parents believed Germany would offer her a better scientific education. But today she was heading home just in time to celebrate Christmas with her parents and dog Lobo in Panguana.

CHAPTER TWO
CHRISTMAS EVE

It is a lightly overcast morning on Christmas Eve 1971. At the Jorge Chávez International Airport in Lima, Peru, clumps of passengers press toward the ticket counters. Summer is beginning in the southern hemisphere, and the holiday adds to the already-buoyant atmosphere. Laughter and excited murmurs fill the air, while presents peek out of bags and purses. Families hug, students gossip, and holiday travelers bargain to get last-minute tickets.

Juliane Koepcke and her mother squeeze through the crowd, eager to make their flight. They are behind schedule and almost didn't get tickets. Juliane had begged her mother to stay one more day in Lima so she could attend the school's *fiesta de promoción*, her high school graduation dance held on the evening of the ceremony. The night was a whirlwind of dancing, laughter, and tearful goodbyes with her classmates. Her mother relented and rebooked their flight.

Now the pair work through the throng of hundreds of people to find their boarding gate. Juliane is wearing a sleeveless, flowered minidress, sandals, prescription glasses, a ring, a watch, and a fashionably cropped head of blonde hair. This is her city attire. When the plane lands in Pucallpa, a midsize town in the Amazon, she'll swap her outfit for rolled-at-the-knees khaki pants, rubber boots, a loose shirt, and a bandanna before continuing the long trek home. Panguana is in a remote area of the Amazon with no direct route. It is accessible only by narrow, unpaved roads, muddy hiking footpaths, and river travel. Only 4x4 vehicles can make it through the deep mud during the rainy season.

Around the gate for LANSA Flight 508, Juliane sees annoyed travelers slumped in chairs, bitterly disappointed they can't get on the plane. A woman pleads for a ticket from an airline agent. She needs to get to a wedding. A frustrated movie crew surrounded by crates of equipment stands dejected. They are unable to get on this flight after their plane was grounded. Juliane knows she and her mother are lucky to get tickets after changing their flight. The passengers form a line and a clerk begins the check-in process.

Juliane and her mother join the queue. Two cheerful American boys her age turn to Juliane and chat about the plane. It is named after a Peruvian hero, Mateo Pumacahua, who was chopped to pieces by the Spaniards. "Hope it doesn't happen to the plane," one boy jokes. The trio smiles. The boys are the children of missionaries who live outside of Pucallpa.

The medium-size Lockheed Electra is filled to capacity with eighty-six passengers. Three pilots and three flight attendants make up the cabin crew. Juliane and her mother settle into their adjacent seats—19E and 19F—in the second-to-last row behind the right wing. Juliane sits by the window. She loves to fly and doesn't want to miss a minute of the scenery. Her mother flashes a tight smile and wedges into the middle seat next to a plump man on the aisle. The man immediately falls asleep and starts a loud, raspy snore.

The Electra speeds down the runway and floats above the capital city. It smoothly breaks through the light blanket of clouds that shroud the city and soars into the blue December sky. Juliane's mother meets her eyes. "It's totally unnatural that such a bird made of metal takes off into the air," she says.

FOLLOW THE WATER

Juliane smiles and then looks out the window. Her mother experienced a flight years earlier when an engine failed and the plane made an emergency landing. It was a frightening ordeal that still haunts her.

The southern hemisphere solstice holiday beckons with a bright, stretching summer. Juliane's life in Lima fades as she contemplates her homecoming. Four hundred fifty miles away from the humming plane, her house on stilts stands on the fringe of the rainforest next to the slow, winding river. Lobo and her father will be on the alert, listening near the banks of the Yuyapichis River for the shrill blast of her mother's whistle that will let her father know they've arrived. She thinks about digging her hands into the German shepherd's thick neck ruff and inhaling the wild smell of his black-blond fur. They will watch Hans's steady figure pole their long canoe across the water. The trio will ferry together to the other shore, a tight-knit family, always relieved and happy to be together.

The seat belt sign dings and turns off. Amid continuing laughter and excited chatter, the seventy-minute flight leaves the Pacific coast shortly after noon and heads over the Andes Mountains. In less than two hours, most passengers will be embraced by family and friends in time for Noche Buena, the Peruvian Christmas Eve celebrations. Hot chocolate mixed with cloves and cinnamon, gifts, roasted turkey, tamales, fireworks,

CHRISTMAS EVE

and the joy of homecoming await the passengers and crew.

The lilt of lighthearted voices rises in the cabin. A burst of laughter trickles back to Juliane and her mother. The stewardesses inch down the aisle in low-heeled pumps and fitted jackets, blue flight caps perched at jaunty angles on their heads. Their faces are fixed into pleased smiles. They serve the buoyant passengers sandwiches and drinks. Juliane and her mother happily nibble the snack. The jubilant mood is contagious.

Juliane watches snowy mountaintops, sharp as saw blades, blur into the horizon. She knows that flying over the Andes Mountains in midday poses challenges to pilots. Unexpected turbulence and drops in altitude can startle passengers. Planes can suddenly lose dozens of feet of elevation. Hot air from the jungle rises to the freezing summits above the tree line to create waves and pockets of unstable air. But today the mountain crossing is smooth. Forty minutes after takeoff, the plane clears the peaks with just a few minor rattles and shakes.

The flight steadily hums over eastern Peru, and Juliane watches the mountains gradually shrink and then transform into a green blanket of rainforest spreading out to the horizon. The plane begins its descent, twenty minutes from landing.

In the cockpit, the pilots' chitchat abruptly halts.

FOLLOW THE WATER

The plane's radar anticipated normal summer showers, but ahead of them a towering black thunderhead knotted together in a violent storm looms menacingly. There was no word on the radio about such severe conditions over the jungle, and the nose of the plane heads directly toward the storm. The pilots decide they are too close to fly around the squall and they will lower altitude to avoid the worst of the storm.

The seat belt light switches on and a stewardess's voice fills the cabin. *Passengers, we inform you that the area of turbulence we are going through is due to a major storm over the Amazon jungle. Fasten seat belts.*

The plane flies straight into the oily black clouds. As if a giant hand flicked a light switch, the interior of the cabin plunges into darkness. A collective gasp of surprise and fear comes from the passengers. Violent eddies of air knock the airplane sideways and up and down and tear at its aluminum outer skin. Juliane's mother clutches her hand, and their eyes meet. "Hopefully, this goes all right," her mother says.

Luggage, cakes, flowers, and packages rain down on the passengers from the overhead compartments. Plates and magazines fly through the cabin, and drinks shower onto heads. Outside Juliane's window, threads of lightning crisscross the sky in wild spiderwebs, and in the bursts of light, she sees the clouds whip and streak by like crazed beasts. In the cabin, the air itself seems black. Passengers call out names, scream, and cry for help. Prayers and pleas to God fill the compartment.

In the cockpit, the flight crew struggles for control. The wind jerks the plane left and right, and they fight against the storm to keep the yoke level and the plane moving forward. The shell of the fuselage shakes as the wind peels and scrapes at its bolts and seams.

Juliane's internal clock stops ticking. She can't tell if ten minutes or ten seconds have passed. All her senses and attention fix on the present as she grips her armrests.

A crack of thunder, and a flash of light explodes outside her window. A bolt of lightning has plowed into the right wing. The brilliant electrical flash blinds her for a moment.

Juliane doesn't see the wing buckle and tear off the plane.

With no right wing, the plane stops struggling and surrenders to the wind. Juliane's vision returns as the passenger cabin dips forward. Above the wails of terror and the rumble of metal ripping apart, her mother's hand tears away from hers. She hears Maria say clearly, "Now it's all over."

The plane lurches into a steep vertical nosedive. The engines scream and roar. The growl and screech of the struggling machines shake Juliane's entire body. She pitches forward, though her seat belt holds her in her seat. She can see straight down the aisle. The cockpit

FOLLOW THE WATER

door flaps open, and the control panels, knobs, and the frantic hands of the pilots are directly below her.

The passenger cabin cracks apart in front of Juliane, and the entire plane crumbles away from her into the storm. Her window, the other passengers, seats, flying packages, everything disappears. For a moment, still belted into her seat, she feels herself suspended in mid-air, in a raging thunderstorm two miles above the Amazon rainforest. Two seats are still attached to hers, but they are empty. The seat belts flap and snap in the wind. Her mother and the snoring man are gone.

The roaring of the engines stops.

She begins to fall.

PLANE FLIGHTS, DISASTERS, AND SAFETY

A plane flies with a delicate balancing act of lift, weight, thrust, and drag. Engines thrust a plane up into the air, and the shape of the wings helps it lift and soar. Pilots must be sure that their plane's weight is balanced and that the thrust of the engines can overcome any drag caused by the plane's structure. They control the plane with a yoke. It's U-shaped and is similar to a steering wheel in a car. The yoke helps the pilot manage the pitch (up-and-down movement) and roll (side-to-side movement) of the plane.

The *Mateo Pumacahua* was a Lockheed L-188 Electra, designed in the 1950s with few safeguards, and the LANSA aircraft company had a poor safety reputation. Under normal circumstances the plane functioned well, and Juliane's plane took off and flew over the Andes Mountains just fine. The trouble began when it flew straight into a giant thunderstorm.

Thunderstorms are frequent near the equator and start on the warm and steamy forest floors. When a day grows warmer in the rainforest, water-saturated air rises into the atmosphere. As the air rises, it cools, causing moisture to condense, or gather, to form clouds. Storms in equatorial rainforests can drop 79 to 394 inches of water per year.

The menacing, dark towers of a thunderstorm are cumulonimbus clouds. The name comes from the Latin language: *cumulus* (heap) and *nimbus* (rain cloud), and they are commonly known as the King of Clouds. These powerhouses develop when smaller clouds band together. They have a base height of 1,100 to 6,500 feet but can extend much higher into the atmosphere. Air movements and particle collisions in the clouds create lightning. Thunder soon follows as the lightning heats the air and it expands. Any cooled air sinks to the ground and causes winds.

Juliane's plane flew into the thunderstorm when lightning was firing. A bolt struck the wing where the fuel was stored, and the tank exploded. The airstream caught the weakened wing and tore it off. Suddenly the plane lost lift and thrust and began to plunge to the ground. Juliane was sitting right behind the wing, and her row popped out into the raging storm. She fell separately from the rest of the plane.

Today, more than one hundred thousand flights take off and land around the world each day, and accidents are very rare. The jumbo jets that transport us around the world have built-in protections that keep us safe in wild weather. Sensors, computers, backup systems, and careful air traffic control keep our flights safe. But what about storms? We can't control the weather, so how do we stay safe if lightning strikes a plane?

Surprisingly, many commercial passenger planes are hit at least once by lightning each year and cope with it very well. It's careful engineering that shields us. You might hear a loud noise or see a flash, but there will be few other effects. Jet fuel is carefully sealed away and there is little chance of the electricity igniting it. Modern fuels use fewer explosive vapors, and every small vent, pipe, or filler cap is designed and then tested to withstand lightning.

Wing tips and the nose of the plane are where lightning likes to attach. The current travels through the aluminum skin and often exits through the tail. Passengers might see lights flicker but feel no electrical charge. The instruments are protected by the metal skin of the plane and built-in surge protectors. This keeps the miles of wires and delicate computer systems safe.

Pilots report lightning strikes, and the ground crew checks all systems and does a visual inspection of the planes before they take flight again. No pilot likes to fly in bad weather, and most pilots of small, personal aircraft avoid flying during thunderstorms. Noncommercial planes have fewer safeguards. This is because noncommercial planes are used for personal travel, recreation, or training. They don't transport cargo or paying passengers.

CHRISTMAS EVE

The wind in Juliane's ears starts as a whisper and builds into a howl as she plummets. She clings to her seat as it begins to twist, spin, and flip like a roller coaster. Her vision blurs as the change in pressure from inside the cabin to exposure at high altitude bursts blood vessels in her eyes.

Juliane passes out.

When she snaps into consciousness again, she's spinning upside down, still hundreds of feet above the ground, hurtling toward the jungle while belted into her seat. Through racing puffs of clouds, she watches the fuzzy jungle floor loom closer. She isn't cold or terrified or panicked, but she feels tremendously lonely. The seat belt digs so painfully into her stomach that it is difficult to breathe. Then her plunge slows. Her chair falls backward and then forward. She watches the densely packed, green foliage come closer and closer in a dizzying, kaleidoscopic spin.

She passes out again.

In the Amazon rainforest, everything green strains for the life-giving energy of the sun. Juliane, unconscious, smashes backward into the crown of the tallest trees, the overstory. She tears into the highest spindly emerging giants, sentinel heads above, and straighter than their juvenile cousins. Branches claw and rake at the empty row of seats, which acts as a sort of cushion between her and the jagged limbs and knife-sharp thorns.

Juliane's fall continues through the treetops of the upper canopy, just below the overstory giants. She hurtles through millions of leaves, stems, and flowers that form the jungle's thick lower canopy. The seats careen and bounce, supported and pushed by the layers of moist vegetation and all that lives in them. She passes through clusters of air plants, orchids, and tree ferns and scrapes through palms with hard, inch-long stickers and spine-stiff fronds. Amazon creepers and liana vines braid around adjoining trees to form a kind of cargo net. Juliane bounces through the tangle, slowing down, cushioned, and sheltered.

She is still in her seat.

The vines give way then, and she shoots through the moist understory of giant ferns, fallen trees, and seedlings. The row of seats pushes through the green bramble of the shrub layer and skids to a stop on the wet forest floor. The seats are now face down, cradling over Juliane. She is still unconscious and strapped into her seat, dangling forward.

Daylight fades.

At some point during the night, she becomes aware of the pressure on her stomach and, semiconscious, unfastens her seat belt. Then she collapses face down on the ground, blacking out again.

TEN THOUSAND FEET

How did Juliane, a slim, seventeen-year-old girl, survive a near two-mile fall that would be like falling from seven vertically stacked Empire State Buildings?

Think of seeds.

The average human falls through the air at 120 to 200 miles an hour. It is difficult to control your body at such a high speed. Moving your limbs at this velocity feels like you're putting your hand outside of a car window while driving fast. The great power and speed of falls from high places make the survival rate close to zero.

Many types of seeds, like maple seeds, have stiff, paper-thin membranes that catch the wind as they fall. These membranes attach to the seed kernel. When the seed breaks free from the tree, the membranes catch the wind and begin to spin the kernel around. The spinning causes lift that counteracts gravity and helps the seed fly. They look like tiny helicopters. Seeds sometimes travel farther than a mile from the parent tree to find their own spots to grow.

Juliane spun to the ground attached to the third seat in her row. The other two empty seats acted like a seed wing. Juliane was the kernel. This initially slowed her fall.

Air is filled with different types of gas molecules. When the sun heats these molecules, they begin to move faster and separate from one another. This heated air is less dense, so it floats up to form thermals: large, lighter, warm streams, or plumes, of air. These thermals rise quickly, some lasting a few seconds, others several minutes. During the storm, thermals from the jungle floor rose into the sky and gave Juliane some additional lift as she fell.

Her seat served as a protective shell as she crashed through the upper canopy. It then fell into a web of lianas—many species of thick vines, just like the ropelike vines adventurers swing on in the movies. These long strands of woody growth crave sunlight. They plant their roots firmly at ground level and then begin winding and stretching up toward the sun, using bushes and canopy trees as ladders to climb, to put their own leaves into sunny parts of the rainforest. Lianas can grow two to three inches a day. Their trunk girth can swell up to twenty-four inches in circumference, the size of sapling trees. The goal is to reach the direct sunlight high in the emergent canopy.

The area of the rainforest where Juliane's seat crashed was thick with liana vines. This network of plants acted like a cargo net, catching the falling row of seats and further slowing its descent to the ground. As the seats tumbled through the network of lianas, they twisted and slowed until they came to a less violent stop on the forest floor.

The combination of science and good luck saved her life.

Juliane lies under the seats on the moist, rotting plant and animal decay that covers the reddish soil. One of her white sandals is gone, and her glasses have vanished. Her watch is still on her wrist. It's ticking.

Startled by the crash, the jungle around her takes a deep, silent breath before its sounds resume: first a

CHRISTMAS EVE

cautious peep, then building back into a throbbing hum of howls, chirps, hisses, and buzzes. Night creeps over the forest, and a heavy rain tattoos the seats until dawn. Juliane sleeps, unaware of the pulsing life around her. She is many miles from Pucallpa, deep in the soul of the untouched, primitive Amazon rainforest.

She hovers in and out of consciousness through the night.

CHAPTER THREE
CHRISTMAS MORNING

Sheets of rain sweep through the forest as Juliane lies immobile, covered by the seats. In the dim gray of early morning, two dreams stitch together, as if her mind is sorting out the shock of the disaster.

She hurtles through a dark room at a low height, careening at high speeds, an engine roar pulsing and throbbing through her body. But she never hits the walls.

Then she feels mud, scum, and liquid clinging to her skin. She needs a bath. "Just get up and go to the bathroom and wash this sticky dirt and filth off," she tells herself. "It's easy. Just get up and go to the bathroom. It's not that far. I'm getting up."

Her decision to get up in her dream alerts her body

CHRISTMAS MORNING

to open her eyes. It's a sunny morning and Juliane understands immediately what has happened. She has crashed into the Amazon jungle and *survived*.

The storm that snatched the plane from the sky has dissipated. Sunlight pushes through the thick leaves and peppers the forest in a golden sheen. She looks around. Above her, hundreds of shades of green glisten and flitter in glowing sunlight, bouncing and dancing on leaves and fronds. The light-infused canopy shimmers and flashes like a living stained-glass window. The light feels familiar.

RAINFOREST LEAVES

Each green leaf in the rainforest is a little factory. Virtually all green plants carry out a chemical reaction called photosynthesis. The process is fueled by sunlight, producing sugar and other molecules that feed the plants and help them grow.

The Amazon has more than 390 billion trees, as well as billions of smaller shrubs, grasses, flowering plants, ferns, and mosses. The number of leaves in the rainforest is astronomical. Each leaf chugs away, creating sugars and removing carbon dioxide (CO_2) from the air.

The shape and texture of Amazon leaves reflect their environment. Approximately 90 percent of rainforest plants have pointy drip tips and a waxy surface. This adaptation channels rainwater quickly off the leaf. If they didn't have drip tips to shed water, they would soon be covered with algae and other growth that would block photosynthesis. The common houseplant philodendron is from the rainforest. Its pointy tips must be avoided when watering to prevent puddles on the floor.

The understory *Coccoloba* plant demonstrates a jumbo-size strategy. It grows ninety-nine-inch-long by fifty-seven-inch-wide leaves in adulthood. This massive surface gives more opportunity for the sun to touch the leaves and for photosynthesis to occur. It's a handy conformation for a plant that is blocked by tall trees from most of the sun's direct rays.

The Swiss cheese plant lives on the dark, lower levels of the rainforest. It has broad leaves with splits and holes. This allows more shafts of sunlight, known as sun flecks, to filter down to its lower, older leaves for photosynthesis.

Several species carry chemical compounds known as alkaloids, which, if eaten, can cause twitching muscles, whole-body spasms, and suffocation. The jolly-looking plants in the *Strychnos* genus, with their reddish fruit and deep green leaves, are one such group of widow-makers. They contain the deadly poison strychnine.

Plant-based Indigenous cultures in the Amazon, like the Jamamadi, gather the toxic resin of strychnine and dip the tips of their arrows into the poison. If the arrow's tip reaches its prey's blood, the prey dies. The active chemical in the plant does have medical uses, but extreme care must be used in extracting it without the toxic compound.

CHRISTMAS MORNING

Everything is wet. Water rolls down the spines of leaves and careens over bark in mini waterfalls, rolling and plopping to the ground. The air itself feels soggy. Juliane draws heavy, thick breaths. The scents, the dankness of rotting leaves, the sun's warmth filtering in to heat the forest floor, the mud filled with decomposing life—all these she knows. They are the same at her home—Panguana. Could Panguana be nearby? Is she near her home?

Juliane gazes up and tries to focus on the tallest trees, shooting up hundreds of feet above her. Her left eye is swollen shut, but through her slightly puffy right eye she senses the familiarity of the solid giants looming over her, some with trunks thirteen feet in circumference. A bleak realization settles in: She's in the rainforest, but far from her home. They had just cleared the Andes Mountains and entered jungle airspace when the storm consumed them. This means she is far from any settlements and Panguana.

There are no human debris around her, no sign of the airplane or its occupants, no sign even of her crash through the leaves and branches. The forest has swallowed the plane and all the people and sealed them in its belly.

Rainwater soaks her clothes and the ground beneath her. She lies in a jigsaw of leaves, moss, and puddles of brown water. Her matted hair sticks to her head, and mud smears her dress, which hangs loosely from her, the zipper on its back halfway torn off. She looks at her feet and sees one white sandal. It is streaked with mud. Her thoughts sort out the grim details. *The airplane crashed, and I survived. Where is my mother? Where is everyone else?*

Juliane places her palms on the earth, eases herself out from under the seats, and stands. The forest immediately disappears into a black whirlpool. She careens forward and falls to her hands and knees. Her head pounds, and her blurred vision worsens. She hears her watch tick and squints at its face. The hands rest on nine o'clock, and the sun tells her it's morning. Exhausted by the smallest of movements, Juliane sinks onto the ground.

Loneliness washes over her. There is no voice calling for her. No one familiar to comfort her. A moment ago, her mother was sitting next to her, grasping her hand, and now she is gone. There are no plane parts or other people lying nearby hurt or even dead. Juliane is the only human in the forest.

She brings herself to her knees and tries to stand again. The forest spins. She stumbles forward, and her mind wavers into grayness. Her legs balance shakily, and she notices a wound on her left calf. It is a deep, wide-open slash into her muscle, with rough edges, but it is not bleeding, and it doesn't hurt.

She shrugs, and her shoulder moves oddly. Her

fingertips trace her right collarbone and feel two ragged edges. She knows that it is broken. She surveys the rest of her body and puts a finger into an inch-deep puncture the size of a button on the back of her arm. Her head spins and feels like it is smothered in cotton.

Juliane feels no pain or concern about the severity of the wounds, but with no warning, a deep, biting anguish and sense of utter abandonment sweep through her. Her legs buckle and she falls to her knees. On all fours she crawls under the seats and peers into the undergrowth.

"Mother! Mama!" she calls and then shouts. No human voice answers. "Mama, where are you?"

Water plops, glistens, and sparkles on the leaves everywhere around her. A profound craving to drink grows in her throat. Her thirst is agonizing, but she hesitates. Her parents have pointed out plants and flowers in the jungle that are poisonous, and she knows a wrong choice could kill her. The most innocent-looking green leaf could hide poison that could paralyze her lungs and suffocate her.

She sees palm trees and leaves of other species she recognizes. She leans into them. She licks the leaves and sucks the moisture carefully into her mouth.

The small drink focuses her thoughts. She stands, keeps her balance, and surveys the dense jungle all around her. In the jungle, everything can start to look the same. She could easily become disoriented and

FOLLOW THE WATER

hopelessly lost. How many times at home in Panguana had her father taught her to walk in the forest with a machete? They notched and hacked lines in the tree trunks to serve as trail markers as they passed, and she always wore rubber boots because of the poisonous snakes.

She considers her one shoe and ripped minidress. Her glasses are gone. She looks at her hands. Her ring is still on her finger. She has no tools. But she knows she must move.

On shaky legs Juliane circles the plane seats again and examines the forest. She selects a broad tree trunk and memorizes its bark and branch locations. With that tree as an anchor, she continues to widen her circles around the seats, scanning the ground and pushing through bushes, looking for anything that might have fallen with her. She yells as loudly as she can, over and over, for her mother and any other survivors. She screams, "Hello! Is there anyone there?!"

Nothing.

She searches until the afternoon and finds only two items buried in the thickets—a bag of fruit candy and a *panetón*, an Italian cake eaten with cinnamon-spiced hot chocolate as a wildly popular Peruvian Christmas treat. The cake is soaked with murky water and mud. It tastes so terrible she throws it away, but she eats three pieces of hard candy and keeps what is left.

CHRISTMAS MORNING

She finds no other food. The jungle is usually rich with fruit and roots. But by December, most fruit has been happily gobbled up by monkeys and tapirs or disappeared into the throats of a billion insects. It's the beginning of the rainy season, when the plants and forest trees soak in rain and nutrients so the fruit cycle will start again. Juliane often watched her father split open bark and hard kernels to find the edible internal parts of plants in stems and branches, but without a knife or a machete, she can't cut through tough plant tissue to get at the food. There is nothing for her to harvest.

She expands her search into wider circles. Her head throbs, and her hearing is still muffled but improving. She strains to hear any human sounds, when a machine hum breaks through the jungle noises. Airplanes are circling above her.

She yells and throws up her arms, but her surge of joy ends as the plane noise dies away. She realizes the searchers can't see her. She is a human dot covered by an ocean of green.

Despair clutches at her. *I will die here. No one will rescue me. They can't see me from the planes. I'm like one of the jungle leaves. Invisible from the air. And how will they find me on the ground? The jungle's immense, and there are no trails here.*

As the sound of the plane engines fades, she remembers her father's patient lessons on how to make a fire from sticks and certain types of rocks. She gazes around at the moist forest floor and the bramble of the shrub layer. The rainstorm soaked every stick and stone. There is no dry fuel for tinder. No amount of rubbing could create the heat needed for a spark or smoldering charcoal.

She hears shifts and rustles in the bushes and spins around but sees no animals. She knows thousands of eyes observe her. If she stays where she is, she will die. She will starve, be attacked by animals, get infected, or perish from the elements. If she hopes to find something to eat and be found herself, she will need to move out of the thick forest. She will have to walk through the jungle and over land where there are no trails. Her only tools for survival are the lessons she's learned from her parents and a molding bag of fruit candy. But she has to find people.

As the day fades into late Christmas afternoon, thousands of frog baritones, tenors, and sopranos swell into a raucous choir of celebration for the coming twilight. Juliane struggles to keep her head clear. The chatter of monkeys high in the canopy top trails down through the leaves. And then under the noise of the creatures she hears a steady tinkling sound. It's gurgling. The noise grows from a dull murmur to sharp plinks. She abruptly realizes it has been there all along, muffled in the haze of her jumbled senses and the noise of the frogs and

CHRISTMAS MORNING

monkeys. *There's water here, a stream, and it's close.* Thirst swells again in her throat.

She follows the sound to a miniature bubbling rivulet that flows over a small stone, and kneels in the mud at the water's edge. Her cupped hands bring water to her lips, but she hesitates. The water is clear and moving over the ground. But still, it could have parasites or bacteria that could kill her. It is unboiled water, and it's impossible to build a fire.

BACTERIA AND VIRUSES

Bacteria are tiny, single-celled organisms, invisible to the naked eye, that exist everywhere on this planet. They were among the first life-forms to live on Earth 3.5 billion years ago, and they are present in almost all living things, including us. They were first discovered in 1676 by Dutch scientist Antonie van Leeuwenhoek. He described them when examining pond water and scrapings from a human tooth. The microscope revealed to him that we humans coexisted with species of heretofore unknown earthlings. Quickly, science learned that we not only coexist with but are vastly outnumbered by them. And that some of them are not our friends.

In our human ecosystem, most bacteria serve us well by helping to digest food (gut bacteria), provide vitamins, and kill disease-causing cells. But other bacteria, like those that cause pneumonia, tuberculosis, and dysentery, for example, have triggered many deaths. In the modern world, antibiotics have averted many such fatalities. Juliane was right to be initially cautious about drinking wild Amazon water.

In our bodies, trillions of microorganisms outnumber our human cells. But because they are so small, the tiny organisms make up less than 3 percent of our body mass. That means a two-hundred-pound adult will carry two to six pounds of bacteria. One of the most bacteria-packed spots *on the outside* of your body? The belly button.

At about five million trillion trillion strong, these single-celled organisms vastly outnumber all other life-forms on Earth. If it were possible to line them up, they would stretch to the limits of the visible universe, some ten billion light-years away.

Bacteria have been with us so long, and so intimately, that some have lodged themselves permanently in our cells. Mitochondria, our cellular energy generators, are descendants of bacteria that were engulfed by larger organisms billions of years ago. Scientists know that the bacteria of the Amazon are diverse and numerous. More than one thousand species of bacteria have been found in a single sample of Amazon River water.

Most bacteria are harmless, and presently scientists are considering using floating bacteria to stimulate snow and rain in parched areas. This could be a tool to fight climate change. Scientists have also engineered *E. coli* bacteria that can act like computers and assemble into a bull's-eye shape on command. Who can imagine what these order-following bacteria may bring?

Viruses are infectious agents with RNA or DNA that can replicate only in the living cells of an organism, often killing the host cell in the process. Viruses are significantly smaller than bacteria and infect all forms of life, including bacteria. They are the most numerous type of biological form and are found almost everywhere on Earth.

The Amazon forest hosts viruses that cause potentially deadly diseases such as leprosy and viral hepatitis. Other well-known examples of virus-caused diseases are AIDS, COVID-19, smallpox, and measles. Destruction of the world's rainforests brings the threat of releasing more deadly viruses into human populations.

Juliane knows infection is one of the greatest perils in the jungle. But aching thirst overwhelms her, and she drinks. The tiny stream also gives her a chance to clean herself. She splashes her face and hair and rubs the mud off her arms and legs. Hope flickers in her mind. She has water to drink. She can walk and she believes her injuries are not so bad.

The rhythmic ripple of the thin stream is a musical score to her thoughts. Moving water is usually safer to drink than standing water, and she remembers her father speaking to her at Panguana. "If you get lost in the jungle and you find flowing water, then stay near it, follow its course. It will bring you to other people."

Everything looks the same in the tangled understory

FOLLOW THE WATER

of the jungle, and water sounds can disappear in the bird and small mammal calls. She could easily get turned around and lost. If only she had her machete. She could hack her way through the jumble of vines or mark her trail. But this thin stream can act like a trail.

Juliane stands up. *There's no sense in waiting here any longer. I'm alone and search planes will never find me.* She decides to follow the water.

She steps into the stream and calculates each step forward carefully. Her right foot with the sandal goes first to feel the mud, wriggling in the silt to flush out water snakes or poisonous frogs. Then the left foot follows. Everything is slick and slippery, so each step is a struggle to find a grip and balance. She teeters onto rocks and slides in oozing plant matter. Her feet tread methodically downstream.

Probe with the sandal on the right foot.

Follow with a barefoot step.

Probe.

Step.

It is difficult to balance with only one shoe, but it protects one of her feet, and she can use that foot to flush danger. She clutches the bag of candy fruit and inches forward.

Instinctively she avoids touching any plants that she does not know, but the water soon flows under dense brush, and she must press through the bramble that blocks her way. She steps slowly, lifting her feet high and placing them gingerly onto decaying leaves and the moldering mounds of plant detritus. A deadly bushmaster could be hiding and ready to strike. Her hands grip at tree trunks and liana vines, wary of any snake that might drape motionlessly in the trees or bullet ants that could cause searing pain.

BULLET ANTS

The most feared creature in the Amazon rainforest can send grown men crashing to the ground, howling in agony, as the pain it inflicts sears through the body, cascading in waves that don't let up. Its local nickname is "twenty-four hours," because that's how long the torment can last. The culprit? An ant.

The bullet ant is one of the largest ants in the world. But it's still just an ant, about the size of a US quarter. An angry bullet ant will clamp down on your skin with powerful mandibles and then inject its venomous stinger, which contains a toxin that affects muscles and nerves. Multiple stings can lead to unconsciousness but are not lethal to humans. The real horror is the intense pain, truly as severe as a bullet wound.

One Indigenous Amazon tribe, the Sateré-Mawé, use bullet ants in a coming-of-age ceremony. Ants are collected and placed in a mixture of water and medicinal leaves that contain a natural sedative. The groggy ants are then woven into large reed gloves that look like oven mitts. When the ants wake up, they are furious. Adolescent boys slip the gloves onto their hands and endure multiple stings. To complete the initiation, the boys must wear the gloves for ten minutes at a time, multiple times over several months. They must not cry out or complain of the pain. This is thought to prepare them for the rigors of adulthood.

Deep in the duff and mud of the rainforest floor, more than half the life found in the jungle squirms, slithers, and bites. Juliane's bare foot is an unprotected target. Snakes and insects could pierce her skin and poison her. The mud sucks at her feet and grabs at her now-brown sandal. She straddles collapsed rotting logs and inches through shreds of decayed bark and desiccated palm fronds. She longs for her rubber boots.

The rivulet grows into a three-foot-wide stream framed by mudbanks. Juliane moves into the center of the stream where the interwoven jungle is thinner. She looks at her watch. It is six o'clock, and the forest is fading into darkness. She decides to wait for the light of morning and finds a mudbank with a clump of brush that can shield her from predators. She inspects the ground for stinging and biting insects before sitting down.

CHRISTMAS MORNING

Juliane sucks on a fruit candy and thinks again about making a fire, quickly dismissing the idea. Every nearby stick, flower, leaf, and branch glistens with water, and humidity hangs in the air.

She draws her legs to her chest, wraps her arms around her knees, and sinks onto the patch of mud. The vanishing light and persistent moisture send shivers across her skin. At least it isn't raining. She thinks of her mother. *I must find her.*

Heavy black sleep flows over her. All around her, insects stretch and flap their wings and begin the business of eating. Juliane lies dreamless, oblivious to the squadron of mosquitoes piercing her skin and drinking her blood.

CHAPTER FOUR
THE SEARCH

While Juliane lies unconscious, she has no idea that hundreds of people are searching for her plane. Meanwhile, in Panguana, Hans prepares for Christmas, expecting the family to gather for a meal, ending with the *panetón* Maria packed in her suitcase. They would exchange gifts. The women would be tired after the days-long journey, but what a sweet reunion it would be. Hans hasn't seen his daughter in months, and she had just graduated from high school. He is anticipating conversations about summer plans and Juliane's future. He is proud of her achievements and that she plans to pursue science. With Maria again at his side, the three of them would plunge back into the study of the forest.

THE SEARCH

Hans is surprised to see a member of the Módena family enter Panguana in the afternoon on Christmas Eve. When he's told that a LANSA plane from Lima to Pucallpa has crashed, Hans confidently expresses doubt that Maria and Juliane could be on the plane. "My wife and daughter can't possibly have been on board that plane," he says, full of conviction. "I specifically told them not to fly with LANSA. My wife never would have set foot on that airplane!" The neighbor leaves the station hoping that his friend is correct.

On Christmas Day Juliane's father wakes and turns on the radio. The radio station obtained a list of the passengers on the plane. He is alone in Panguana as he listens in stunned silence as Maria's and Juliane's names are read. He quickly travels to an airstrip near Pucallpa and stays glued to a short-wave radio waiting for the latest news from the rescue teams.

When air traffic control lost contact with LANSA Flight 508 in the late afternoon on Christmas Eve, the largest land and air search mission in the history of Peru began. The Pucallpa airport immediately contacted the Peruvian Air Force about the missing plane, and Air Force Commander Manuel del Carpio takes charge of the search teams. For most of the passengers on the flight, Pucallpa was their destination. Anxious families and friends stream into the airport desperate for news.

All Peru knew that Líneas Aéreas Nacionales, or

FOLLOW THE WATER

the LANSA company, was notorious for accidents. People joked that "LANSA *se lanza de panza,*" or "LANSA lands on its belly." The company's most recent disaster happened only a year prior. That tragedy took the lives of forty-nine American students on a trip to the ancient Incan ruins of Machu Picchu near Cuzco, Peru. Officials attributed the cause of that crash to pilot error and improper maintenance.

Maria had been pressured by Juliane to stay another night. If they had not gone on the LANSA flight, they wouldn't have been able to fly out until the next day or two, interrupting their plans for Christmas. As it was, Maria was impatient to get home and decided to risk it. On Christmas Eve they walked on the tarmac to the boarding stairs unaware that this was also LANSA's only remaining plane. All the others had either crashed or were unflyable.

Commander del Carpio's task is daunting. The last verbal communication with the pilots of Flight 508 indicated that the flight path was unchanged, but when they entered the thunderstorm, radar tracking of the plane abruptly vanished. The air traffic controllers have no idea exactly where the plane went down.

The searchers plot a trapezoid shape over pristine rainforest where Flight 508 was most likely to have crashed. Military and private search planes with spotters comb the forest from the skies, and a ground team

THE SEARCH

starts to hack through the walls of growth to reach the suspected area.

The jungle yields no clues. The rainstorms that torment Juliane on the forest floor also shorten the flight time for the searchers, and when the weather does clear, a lingering fog shrouds the treetops. Beyond that, the dense canopy makes any plane crash debris virtually invisible from above.

While the weather is abysmally rainy, this, and the heat, will not immediately kill a person. There is plenty of water. The enemy is time. The longer any possibly injured survivors stay in one place where they can't be seen from the air, the more surely they will die. Injuries will worsen, and wound and insect-bite infections will set in. They'll be in danger from foraging animals, and unless they can find food, they will starve.

Ground crews forge on, but rain and walls of tangled vines, plants, and trees prevent meaningful progress. They grapple with an average daily rainfall of five inches, and when the weather clears, the oppressive heat and blazing sun beat down on them. The rain brings mudslides that also thwart the efforts. In a sad occurrence, Adolfo Saldaña, the father of one of the passengers, is killed in a traffic accident on a mud-ridden, potholed road while bringing food to support the rescue teams.

Meanwhile, more families gather in Pucallpa and

demand answers. Both Peruvian and international press corps descend on the city. The families wait in desperation while reporters dig and poke for any clues.

Loved ones cling to any piece of information they hear. The parents of the two American boys who chatted with Juliane are part of the Wycliffe missionary community, devoted to translating the Bible into Indigenous languages. Their group had five members of the settlement on Flight 508, including the boys and the parents of two children who had skipped the trip to Lima because of a case of chicken pox. Because traveling in the jungle was so difficult on the trails, the missionary group decided in the 1950s to purchase their own planes and train local pilots. They send three of their own small planes into the sky, hunting for the crash and survivors.

Unofficial sources spread false hope through erroneous newspaper reports. Pucallpa is rife with gossip. Anonymous letters are sent to the authorities, cruelly claiming sightings of the wreck and planes falling from the sky. People in a nearby mountain range report a sighting of the wreck. Workers in the jungle tell of a low-flying plane the day of the crash. Bright lights and an explosion are reported. These rumors confuse the search efforts further. Commander del Carpio threatens arrest and interrogation for false reports, but the unfounded reports persist.

This confusion fills the families with fear and

THE SEARCH

anguish. Two sons have not come home to their parents. A mother is inconsolable over the loss of her three daughters. A father waits for his wife and five-year-old son. In several cruel twists of fate, one passenger won his ticket in a contest, and another enthusiastically boarded the plane after a last-minute cancellation opened up a seat for him. In all, ninety-two daughters, mothers, sons, fathers, and friends have disappeared into the green wilderness of the Amazon jungle.

Hans remains hopeful but his anger grows. He clashes with the search officials and believes that not enough is being done. He is a man who gets things done and pushes ahead through adversity. His perception that the efforts are lackluster is clouded by his desperation. Maria could be alive and waiting for rescue. And Juliane is so young. He doesn't give up hope.

CHAPTER FIVE
FOLLOW THE WATER

The jungle dawn pulls Juliane out of an ink-black sleep. Above her, the dome of trees and plants brightens with the daylight. Sunlight breaks through the crowns of the tallest trees, but the streambank rests in cool shadows. Brown tree trunks trim the shore, and broad fan-like leaves knit together over the water. The birds and insects resume their cacophonous chant.

Juliane brushes soil and leaves off the top of the stream, dips her hand in, and drinks. The water does nothing to quell the despair settling in her heart. She counts her sweets and eats a few to push down her hunger. Her fingers adjust the remaining sandal securely onto her right foot. *I've got to get out of here.* The thought repeats and amplifies in her mind. *I've got to move.* She scans the jungle around her for signs of the crash. A sign of people. Her mother. There is nothing.

Her legs are shaky, but she manages to rise and continue in the stream. Probe with the sandal on the right foot. Follow with a barefoot step.

Every few yards it grows wider, and the banks enlarge a few inches. The forest leaves drift back from over the water, and the vines are now too far for her to grab for support. High above her, howler monkeys skim the upper canopy that still covers the stream. Their low, guttural sounds carry for miles in the forest.

A small creek flows into a larger one. There I can find help. There I can find people.

The daytime insects discover her. Butterflies and crickets land on her matted blonde hair. Stingless sweat flies cluster in droves on her cheeks and forehead to drink her perspiration. She ignores them except to calmly flick them away when they creep too close to her nostrils or eyes.

Probe.

Step.

Animals creep out of the brush to drink from the stream. Tapirs, brocket deer, martens, and red titi monkeys note her presence without alarm and move on. A grim realization occurs to her. *They have no fear because they've never seen people. There is no one anywhere near here.*

She passes a Goliath birdeater spider tucked into tree

FOLLOW THE WATER

bark. Its legs stretch wide—twelve inches from tip to tip—trembling menacingly at her. She knows it is aggressive and can catch and devour small birds and reptiles. She remembers neighbors at Panguana sometimes ate the spider. But she has no fire to cook it, or banana leaves to wrap it. *It can pounce and bite me, and the bite is worse than a wasp's sting.* She moves guardedly past it. The spider stays near its burrow.

GOLIATH BIRDEATER SPIDERS

If you think spiders are small, think again. The Goliath birdeater is the world's biggest tarantula—so large, it's been compared to the size of a puppy. With a leg span reaching nearly a foot and weighing in at six ounces, this eight-legged beast prowls the rainforest floor like a hairy, creeping tank.

Covered in russet-brown to black hair, the Goliath birdeater relies on its fuzzy coat for more than just warmth. Since it's nearly blind, those fine hairs help it sense the smallest vibrations in the air. Its eight legs are just the start—near its mouth it has extra feelers called pedipalps, which help it grab food and even assist in mating. But the real showstoppers are its massive fangs, nearly two inches long—longer than a cheetah's claw. Though its venom isn't deadly to humans, a bite would still feel like a nasty wasp sting.

Deep in the rainforests of northern Peru, the Goliath birdeater rules its underground burrow. Unlike some of its web-spinning cousins, it prefers to lurk in silk-lined tunnels, waiting for the perfect moment to strike. Despite its fearsome name, the birdeater doesn't snack on birds very often. It's an opportunistic hunter, happily feasting on worms, insects, frogs, lizards, and even the occasional mouse. When it captures prey, it drags it back to its burrow, injects venom, and begins its gruesome feast—liquefying the insides and slurping them up like a horror-movie smoothie.

The Goliath birdeater isn't just a hunter—it's also an expert in self-defense. When threatened, it creates an eerie hissing sound by rubbing its legs together, loud enough to be heard from fifteen feet away. If that doesn't scare off an attacker, it flicks tiny, barbed hairs into the air, which can cause intense irritation, leaving an enemy itchy, teary, and full of regret. As a last resort, it rears up on its hind legs, fangs bared, making sure any predator knows it picked the wrong spider to mess with.

The Goliath birdeater has a surprisingly long life—at least, if it's female. A well-fed female can live up to twenty years, while males rarely make it past six.

In parts of South America, locals roast Goliath birdeaters over an open flame, carefully singeing off the irritating hairs before wrapping them in banana leaves and cooking them to crispy perfection. The taste? A little like shrimp.

Small springs join the growing stream, and the forest forces the water to flow in a winding route. As the morning passes, Juliane follows the snakelike switchbacks of the water. She crawls over tree trunks and squeezes through branches. The sun crests high in the sky. She wills herself to advance and not stop to rest.

Probe.

Step.

In the afternoon she rounds a bend to discover an airplane propeller and engine in the center of the stream. The massive turbine is crushed and covered in oil. One of its propellers hangs limply to the ground. On one side is a long slash of scorched metal. *This must be the engine I saw outside my window. The lightning must have struck the plane here.* She steadies herself with a hand on the twisted engine and looks around. There is no other sign of her plane. But above her, on the other side of the tree canopy, she hears the hum and cough of another engine.

A search plane.

She screams and waves her arms. A brief flash of sun on the plane's wings blinks through the branches, and then the sound drifts away. Juliane welcomes an oddly hopeful feeling. *I'm not so badly hurt. Others might have survived the crash. Mother. And they're looking for us.* She moves on.

Probe.

Step.

The jungle terrain turns hilly and the streambanks grow higher. Soon hundred-foot-tall walls of woven jungle enclose her. The water stretches broader and deeper, now reaching above her knees. She continues until dusk and then finds a stump near the water against which she can lean for the night. The sweltering dusk quickly yields to the black jungle night. She knows she can count on twelve hours of sunlight at the equator, but twilight is short and the forest darkens rapidly to twelve hours of darkness.

Now thoughts of her mother and the impossibility of her plight tumble and twist in Juliane's head. *I have to find her. How could I survive this? Others must be here. I must find the other survivors.* Slowly her mental images blur. Her body rests, and her mind slips into sleep.

A storm gathers. Rolls of thunder vibrate over the trees, and the rain pelts her skin. Thousands of leaves drop millions of thin streaks around her. The earth under her is saturated with moisture seeping from the jungle floor to the stream. Giant raindrops plop into the water, sending intersecting rings across its surface. A cold wind whips the trees. She huddles on the bank, shivering and wavering in and out of a weary sleep. It rains all night. She's relieved that the rain deters the mosquitoes.

The dawn brings sun and warmth. The umbrella of trees has thinned slightly, allowing more light to reach the forest floor. Juliane counts her remaining candy and eats a few for her breakfast. She steps cautiously into the water and wrestles through the snags of fallen trees. The sediment and muck pull at her feet and her one sandal. Her cadence resumes.

Probe.

Step.

The river swells wider and the water rises up to her thighs. A soft breeze helps scatter some flies off her face, and then she freezes. Around a bend in the river she hears the pounding flap of powerful wings. The first beats are long and slow. The sound intensifies into urgent flaps and then relaxes into a shudder. Something is settling down.

Then she hears a high-pitched, burping call. *RyupRyup-Yup.*

King vultures.

KING VULTURES

These experts at others' misfortune are the largest carrion-eating birds of the Amazon. They don't hunt live prey but soar above the rainforest scanning for dead animals to eat. If they spot a sick or injured creature, they wait patiently nearby, or circle above it, waiting for it to die.

Their wings have a six-foot span and are edged by black flight feathers. All flying birds enjoy a lift from rising air, but these vultures rule the sky. Their long, flat wings surf the warm thermals as they glide and soar in the air. Once above the canopy, they rarely flap their broad wings during flight. A slight twitch of flight feathers or shift in wing position can catch a thermal and propel a bird thousands of feet up into the sky.

The vultures' keen sense of smell can pinpoint a dead mouse buried under leaves far below, and sharp, straw-colored eyes spot animals struggling miles in the distance.

Other scavengers often wait for the king vulture to arrive. Its hooked beak and long, razor-sharp talons can tear into a tough hide, making it easier for smaller animals to reach the meal. These vultures also have built-in defenses against the dangers of their diet. Their bald orange-brown heads and necks help prevent bacteria from clinging to their feathers, and their strong stomach acids destroy harmful toxins in rotting meat.

After feeding, king vultures take time to clean up. They use their beaks to remove scraps of flesh, straighten their feathers, and then stretch their wings in the sun. This not only dries their plumage but also warms them up for their next flight—rising into the sky in search of their next meal.

As the daughter of an ornithologist, Juliane is well aware of what the heavy flap of the wings means as she rounds the river bend. Her gut wrenches with dread. *God, no. Don't let it be my mother.* She forces herself to move forward, shivering in the hot sun and fearing what the bend in the river will reveal.

Probe.

Step.

Then she recognizes a row of three seats on the riverbank, just like hers, detached from the plane, with three passengers still strapped in by seat belts. But instead of being cradled by the seat backs, this trio hit the ground headfirst. They were three adults, two men and a woman, and their combined weight across the row of seats made it impossible for them to catch the thermal currents.

Juliane stops, stricken. For the first time, she feels icy fear wash through her. There is death in the jungle, and she might not survive. Her heart pounds in her ears. She steps out of the water and edges closer to the seats. A short, raspy huff filters down from overhead. Three king vultures have lined up on a low tree branch, watching her every move. They are patient participants in the dismal trade of death. They know Juliane will move on and the bodies will stay, and they will be ready when she leaves.

What if it's my mom?

She tears a small branch off a tree and creeps up to the woman's body. The foot has no shoe and Juliane stares at its shape, expecting to recognize it. Her stick lifts the foot gently, and bright nail polish flashes on the toenails in the filtered sunlight.

Juliane drops the stick and draws a jerky breath. *This*

FOLLOW THE WATER

is not my mother. Not with those painted toes. Her huge sense of relief is followed by the understanding that this woman could not possibly be her mother. The thought slipped into her mind so easily, so obviously, and yet—*Why did I even think that? It never could have been her. She was sitting right next to me on the plane. Why didn't I realize that?*

Around the row of seats, a few chunks of metal debris litter the soil and thickets. There are no other people. On the tree branch, the vultures flutter, jostle, and shift position, eager for their meal. Juliane turns back to the water and continues down the center of the river before the vultures begin their work. She hears the whisper of their wings behind her and the hum of the search planes above.

I must hurry.

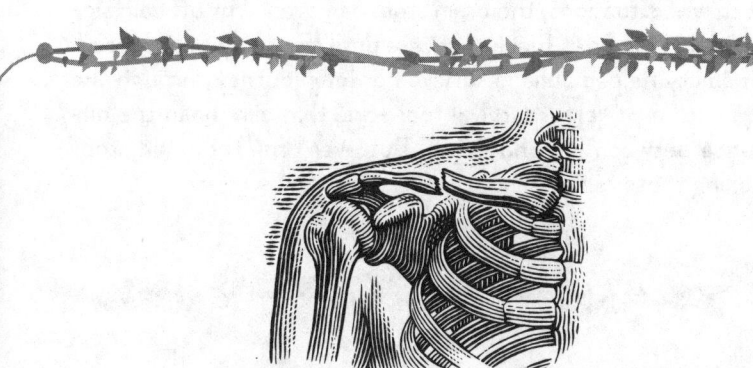

WHY DIDN'T JULIANE FEEL PAIN?

Surviving a plane crash and days in the jungle should have been unbearably painful. But Juliane felt no pain at all, at least at first. Even though she had serious injuries, like a broken collarbone, deep cuts, and a spine injury, she kept moving. She was focused on one thing: survival. The pain didn't fully hit her until she was finally safe and getting medical care.

Stress can also cloud judgment, making obvious facts seem uncertain or distorted. When the brain is overwhelmed by fear or panic, it can jump to conclusions or struggle to process information logically.

Juliane's experience isn't unusual. In life-threatening situations, the brain can block pain and emotions to help a person survive. Scientists call this trauma-induced pain suppression, and it happens for several reasons.

When the body is in danger, the brain has built-in survival tricks to help. It releases endorphins, natural painkillers that temporarily block pain, and pumps out adrenaline to keep a person alert and moving, even when injured. Some people feel emotionally numb, as if they're watching from the outside or forgetting parts of what happened—this is the brain's way of preventing overload. In extreme situations, the brain stem can even shut off pain signals, making injuries feel less severe until the danger has passed. This ability helped Juliane survive her long journey through the jungle. It's a powerful survival tool—one that can mean the difference between life and death. But over time the brain stops blocking those feelings.

CHAPTER SIX
THE DAILY STRUGGLE

One day follows the next for Juliane. Every day near the equator is the same, with twelve hours of sunlight and twelve hours of night, year-round. Slender rays of dawn break through the tangle of leaves at six each morning. The sun sets at six at night. Time crawls in between as she fixates on her steps. She moves through the murky water in a shuffle, carefully avoiding a fall.

Probe.

Step.

Minutes roll into hours. Hours creep into days. Her body wants to stop and stretch out on the streambank. She forces herself to go on. The constant sameness of the forest is mind-numbing. The base layer of insect droning is overlaid with the peeps and croaks of frogs and the songs and shrieks of birds. Only the occasional buzz of the search planes breaks the monotony of the deep forest.

She finishes the last of her candy, and by the fifth day she is ravenous. She covets the edible palms surrounding her, but without a knife, she cannot get to their nutritious centers. The liana vines store fresh, clean water, and she longs for her machete to break through the outer husks. She drinks water from the growing stream every time she rests. *This will help fill my stomach. There are no people here, so I can't get dysentery from human waste.* She pushes away thoughts of parasites and of her parents boiling pots of water at Panguana.

Juliane's thoughts linger over the foods she loves. She imagines the simplest of meals with mouthwatering relish. A piece of toast slathered corner to corner with butter and sweet jam. A cool chocolate milkshake topped with whipped cream. A fried egg.

She dreams of her favorite dish, *papas a la Huancaína*, a steamed, flaky potato dish smothered in a creamy yellow farmer-cheese sauce, surrounded by olives and boiled egg slices. She can taste the brush of garlic and the just-so amount of the powerful Peruvian ají pepper.

The rain eases up occasionally, and brilliant stars and the Milky Way peek through the curtain of leaves.

THE DAILY STRUGGLE

The moon is a white disc in the night sky, just out of reach on the other side of the treetops. Rain clouds race under its glow, and the pale light draws long, dreary shadows across the water.

The nights torture her. When she sighs in relief at a pause in the rain, the insects launch their attack. She can brush off soft moths and night crickets, but the hordes of mosquitoes are impossible to escape. Her skin is covered with swelling, itchy bumps. She buries her head in her arms each night, trying to fall asleep as soon as possible.

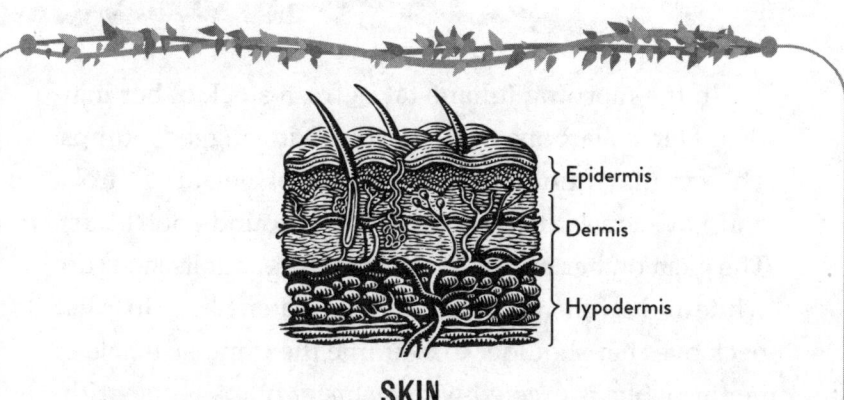

SKIN

The skin is the body's largest organ. It covers about twenty-two square feet on an average adult. It's also hefty, making up 15 percent of a person's total weight. It's the body's armor. But it has some weak spots.

Skin has three main layers, the outer epidermis, dermis, and hypodermis. The layers hold in moisture and defend the body from injury and infection. We navigate through the physical world with the help of skin telling us when things are too hot or cold.

When an insect bites, human skin reacts by filling those areas with histamines, a chemical the body produces to fight infection and help you heal. But histamines also cause swelling, inflammation, and maddening itchiness.

While moisture is good for the skin, too much causes maceration, where the epidermis softens and breaks down. Soak too long in a bath and your skin turns wrinkly: That's maceration. Because Juliane was in the water several hours a day, the outer epidermis around her wounds whitened, and healing slowed.

In the morning Juliane takes fresh stock of her injuries. Her collarbone still has the odd, ragged bumps. The circular puncture on the back of her arm throbs and is viciously itchy, but the other wounds don't hurt. The gash on her leg is still not bleeding, but its sides are white and swollen from days in the water. She cranes her neck over her shoulder to examine the dime-size hole in her arm. She is greeted with a cluster of maggots writhing in the open sore. Flies have laid eggs in the wound, probably while she slept, and now hundreds of larvae burrow into her body. She can feel the white bugs move as they eat into her flesh, but the lesion doesn't bleed. This means the maggots have carved into muscle, where there are fewer blood vessels.

SCREWWORM FLIES

The most likely suspect of Juliane's maggot infestation is the New World screwworm fly. An adult female is about the size of a common housefly. She looks for an open wound in a human or animal host to lay her clutch of eggs, which can number in the hundreds. The host provides a warm, moist home as well as a food source. If a wound is not available, the flies will lay eggs near the ears, nose, or anus of a host. Several flies may have the opportunity to deposit eggs in the same wound. Juliane was most likely the victim of multiple egg-laying sessions.

These eggs hatch into ravenous, cream-colored larvae known as maggots. The young dive headfirst into the flesh of the host, burrow as far as they can, and begin eating. Most species of fly maggots target dead and rotting flesh. The screwworm fly is unusual in that it also digs into healthy muscle. The larvae have small spines on each body segment that look like screw threads. They use these to anchor themselves to their host. Maggot activity can open a pocket in the flesh and is extremely painful.

After about a week, the larvae drop off the host onto the forest floor. There they tunnel into decaying leaf matter to reach the first layer of topsoil. In the brown dirt, the whitish worms develop into pupae, with a protective covering, and then turn brown. Over time they turn into flies and leave their pupa cases.

As of 2025, the screwworm fly has been eradicated in the United States. This is good news for ranchers, as livestock are especially vulnerable to the flies. They will attack a baby calf's navel area at birth, as well as any sores caused by ear tagging. The flies' assaults on livestock can cost millions of dollars a year. For this reason, scientists are ready to flood any known screwworm fly populations with males who cannot reproduce, reducing the chance for offspring and disrupting the flies' life cycle.

Juliane takes off her ring and bends the metal into makeshift tweezers. The instant she touches the sore, the maggots dive deeper into her arm. She probes again with the buckle of her watch with no luck. The creatures aren't forced to the surface, and there is no way to get them out. *The maggots aren't going to kill me right away. I'm their host, and parasites don't always kill their hosts. But the wound might get infected.* She quells a wave of nausea and gazes at the dirty water. She stands up. *I'll think about it later. I've got to get out of here.*

Juliane fashions a walking stick to help keep her balance. She pokes the branch into the deepening water and stirs the bottom before she places her sandaled foot in front of her. Freshwater stingrays lurk in the mud, and a puncture and infection from their powerful stingers would end her trek and her life. Her feet slide over rocks and sink into the treacherous silt. Each step becomes a ponderous effort, but she moves forward, trancelike, concentrating, one foot after the next.

Probe.

THE DAILY STRUGGLE

Step.

From the jungle tangle comes the sound of a low smoker's cough, and then a buzzing call rings out. Hope floods Juliane. She knows this sound so well! Her mother studies the hoatzin, the bird responsible for this tuneless cry, and told her that they nest on the edges of large rivers. The birds flutter and call out. Juliane hobbles faster. *There must be a large river nearby.*

FLYING COWS

Life on the Amazonian rivers is a noisy, perilous affair for the hoatzin, known for its large body, small head, and deep growling coughs and huffs. Small family flocks raise chicks in nests that are built over rivers. When predatory monkeys or snakes attack, the chicks drop into the water to escape. They swim underwater, flapping their wings like penguins. When all is clear, they creep up branches and tree trunks, climbing with hooked claws on their wings, back to the safety of the nest.

In all the bird kingdom, only a few birds follow a strictly vegetarian diet; while many eat seeds or sip nectar, they will not pass up a tasty protein treat of insects or meat. The hoatzin is a rare exception to this rule, as it devours a strict diet of leaves and the occasional fruit.

Many bird species' digestive systems have a crop—a muscular chamber in which food begins to break down, often with the help of sharp pebbles the bird ingests. The hoatzin's ridged, double-chambered crop hosts unique bacteria and acts like an extra stomach. It grinds and ferments vegetation into smaller pieces before sending the meal on to the hoatzin's actual stomach, no pebbles necessary. While the birds don't regurgitate and rechew their food like cows (an act called "chewing the cud"), they do have the same smelly methane burps, a byproduct of the fermentation. Locals in the Amazon know the hoatzin as the stink bird.

Juliane turns a bend to see her stream join a large current winding ahead into the distant forest. This new river is more than thirty feet wide, and the trees can't arch all the way across the water. The hot eye of the sun blazes above. Enormous white cotton-ball clouds crowd the sky as she gladly emerges from the cave-like forest.

But her hopes crumble when she inspects the confluence of the two waterways. Her stream ends in a massive logjam. Broken trees, driftwood, and palm fronds filled with treacherous thorns and stickers clump together in a thick pile. They form a solid wall in the water, stretching from shore to shore, with dense brambles lining the banks. Juliane can barely see over the blockade, and

THE DAILY STRUGGLE

there seems to be no possible way to climb through to the open water. Every scrap of her experience and knowledge tells Juliane to stay on the water and not try to get around the blockage on land. Everything looks the same once you step into the rainforest. No paths exist. The sound of the placid river will get lost in the jungle's noise. She could easily get turned around and wander in circles. She is exhausted and losing energy. And a jaguar could be eyeing her right now. But she must get by the dam of logs.

JAGUARS

The next time you pet a kitten, imagine the jaw power of a jaguar, its Amazonian relative. This jungle feline has the strongest bite of all the big cats. Its short, powerful jaw and specialized teeth create enough pressure to crush a bowling ball. Jaguars rely on this strength to pierce tough turtle shells and grind the bones of their prey.

These elusive cats live beneath the dense forest canopy. Their tawny coats, patterned with dark rosettes—broken rings with spots inside—blend seamlessly into the dappled light of the jungle, providing perfect camouflage for a stealthy hunter. Females typically give birth to one to four cubs, with two being the most common. The young remain with their mother for about two years, during which they play, learn to hunt, and travel by her side, before setting out on their own.

Jaguars are secretive and keenly aware of their surroundings. When they hear humans approaching, they can slip into cover and observe from just a few feet away, unnoticed. Unfortunately, as urban and agricultural expansion pushes deeper into wild lands, conflicts between people and jaguars increase. Though attacks on humans are rare, they can happen—especially when someone unknowingly trespasses into jaguar territory. Juliane never saw a jaguar, but undoubtably, they saw her.

She scrambles onto the closest trunk. Her shoeless foot and bare hands struggle for a hold. Thorns slash her skin. Branches whip her face. Snags grab at her legs. She slips back down into the water. She knows she doesn't have the energy to scale the mound. The large river, just over the pile of bramble, flows lazily, uninterested in her success or failure. It is the road home. She looks at the curtain of jungle on the banks and decides to risk it.

Juliane scrabbles slowly through liana vines, trees, and bushes. It takes hours to advance even a few yards into the web of snarled greenery. A massive, dense stand of wild cane, *caña brava*, stands stiff and firm; its arrowed

THE DAILY STRUGGLE

leaves attack her skin. She pries the lashing stems and branches apart with her hands. Her muscles ache. She leans forward and pushes and pulls at the wall of vegetation. Her small body slips through the holes and green tunnels she creates in the thickets.

The persistent rough calls of the hoatzin and the sound of search planes give her a sense of hope, even euphoria. She battles the tangled cane stalks without stopping.

When she finally breaks through the last of the undergrowth, she steps onto the bank of the larger river. She stares downstream at the milk chocolate–colored ripples, and her heart sinks. Palm fronds and logs crowd the surface. *People can't navigate this river in boats. I have much farther to go.*

A search plane again flies directly over her. She shouts and waves her arms, but the plane soars onward, a fading dot. Suddenly she's filled with a hot fury. *How can they simply turn around now that I've finally reached an open stretch of water after all these days!* Her burst of angry emotion is followed by a steep slide into despair. Then a cold fear washes over her. She realizes with a new clarity how very alone she is and how great the distance between herself and rescue. But out of the roller coaster of feelings, steady thoughts return. *Where there's a river, people cannot be far.* Her father's words return to her. *Follow the water.*

FOLLOW THE WATER

Juliane steps off the sandbank. Her father's words repeat over and over in her head like a mantra. *Where there's a river, people cannot be far.* She strips another branch to probe for sinkholes and stingrays and steps into the water.

Probe.

Step.

Each step she takes, the water rises higher, until her feet no longer touch the riverbed. She relaxes into the center of the river and floats on her stomach with the current until her hands can grab small floating logs as crude life preservers. She steers clear of the larger bobbing rafts of matted vegetation. She's never swum in such a deep, fast-flowing wild river, but she broke through the *caña brava* and she is moving. Hope surges through her.

The following days melt together. The river flows quietly, with few rapids. Juliane grasps the skinnier logs and kicks her legs or floats like a leaf in the warm water, letting the current steadily propel her. *If only I had a boat to navigate through the river*, she thinks. She knows how to travel in boats. She knows how to sit still, not stand or move without thinking. But, for now, she floats.

While she rests on the riverbank, the cloudless night sky unveils the vast treasures of the universe. Billions of stars stud the black nights, sweeping over her head in dazzling pinpoints of white light. Under the expanse of the heavens and surrounded by miles of jungle, she

THE DAILY STRUGGLE

realizes hers is the only human heartbeat for miles. A deep longing lodges in her chest. She thinks about her mother and wonders if she's already been rescued. She imagines that both her parents must be looking for her.

Dawn brings the sun, now a less welcome visitor. On sunny days the rainforest heats into a steamy sauna. Hours of floating in the river turn her fingers and feet as wrinkled and puckered as raisins. Her fair skin is helplessly exposed to the scalding sun. Red, swelling blisters cover her arms, legs, and shoulders.

The only relief comes at sunset, when Juliane hauls herself up onto the sandy banks for the night. She tucks herself against a tree trunk or in a thicket of brush and pulls large leaves over her as a blanket. Her burned skin sends feverish chills through her body. She's worked hard swimming, and her stomach begs for food.

In the river habitat, new sounds join the nightly serenade. The padding of paws and the sound of breaking twigs encircle her as she rests. Deep panting, growls, and snorts hover close by, masked by the jungle's green wall. Juliane silently rises into a crouch on the sand if need be. If the sounds come too close, she speaks or coughs, frightening the unseen animals away.

During the day, cold-blooded caimans sun on the riverbanks in groups of two or three. In the early morning they are groggy. They need to warm up to get moving. She floats by silently without them noticing. In the afternoon the warm, alert reptiles react instantly to her presence. They spy her bobbing body, rise on their stubby legs, and run directly toward her. They dive underwater and thrash nearby. "Caimans always run into the water when they're startled," her father told her. "They're not after you; it's a flight mechanism. Don't splash or try to swim away. You'll look like prey." The giant reptiles dive directly under Juliane, and she wills herself to hold still as they swim by her with their rough, leathery skin.

CAIMANS

Caimans are the ultimate survivors. Their ancestors rode out the asteroid strike that is presumed to have extinguished the dinosaurs sixty-five million years ago. Now these heat-seeking creatures are an apex predator in the Amazon basin rivers. Juliane encountered the spectacled caiman, a smaller member of the alligator family. Males can grow up to eight feet long and weigh more than eighty pounds. Individual caimans are known to live thirty to forty years in the wild, and up to forty years in captivity.

Like all reptiles, caimans are cold-blooded and sluggish until their temperatures rise as they are warmed by the sun. Adult caimans eat fish, mammals, and occasionally sheep or young cattle. They don't seek out humans as prey, but when surprised or hunted, caimans are responsible for deadly attacks on humans every year.

Human hunting and misuse of natural resources have also failed to drive them into extinction. Scientists attribute their low caloric needs, physical toughness, and adaptability as key to their survival.

One windless morning on the shore, a soft squawk wakes Juliane. She opens her eyes. A baby caiman sniffs the air around her nose, mere inches away. Its mouth opens and closes, revealing a snow-white row of miniature fangs. Juliane raises her head slowly and sees a clump of five-inch-long, leather-skinned babies staring at her. In the water, another two heads wriggle her way.

"The most dangerous position you can be in in nature is if you threaten young," her father told her.

Juliane looks down the sandbank. *There she is.* The mother caiman's head turns gradually, and then the glassy green eyes with their coal-black diamond-shaped pupils fix on her face. Juliane's heart pounds. The five-foot caiman is not fully warmed up and eases slowly onto her legs.

Juliane rolls quickly into the water and escapes in the current.

FOLLOW THE WATER

The tropical sun bears down on her. Her unprotected skin cracks and bleeds. When she touches her shoulders, her fingers come away with blood. Each day it's harder to get up, enter the water, and keep going. She doesn't realize it, but eight days have passed since the crash. A new year has begun, and she has traveled over a hundred miles by land and water.

Then she finally sees it. A roof. Smoke. People. Laughter. Chickens clucking.

A feeling of joyful elation and huge relief surges through her. *I'm rescued! At last. I made it.*

"I'm here! I'm here," she shouts, and paddles furiously to the shore. She can see the village homes grouped together, the people outside, and the wisps of smoke trailing up into the sky. Children are laughing and playing soccer. She staggers to a stand on the shore, waving her arms.

And it's gone. The smoke evaporates into heat waves, and the rooftops are palm fronds. The people are merely waving reeds, and the laughter came from a mob of parrots. The children disappear. She is hallucinating.

While Juliane is moving through the river and jungle, trying to find her way home, her father, Hans, struggles with sleepless nights, haunted by the thought that his wife and daughter flew on an airline with a fleet of accident-ridden vessels. He waits desperately for news, sitting at the nearby airstrip and listening to the radio,

THE DAILY STRUGGLE

hoping for a breakthrough. But day after day, the news is the same—search crews are still out there, but there's no sign of the wreckage or survivors.

Hope begins to fade as the days stretch on. The weather clears briefly, expanding the search, but no new information surfaces. One report suggests the plane might have made an emergency landing, but it's a fragile hope. By the tenth day, reality is setting in for the families—despite all the effort, it's looking less likely that anyone survived.

At the Pucallpa airport, the families continue to gather, but the crowd of reporters has thinned. The story has lost its dramatic edge. There's nothing more to report except the absence of the plane. The search continues, but the jungle holds its secrets, leaving only a haunting emptiness. The search becomes a recovery mission, and a new, high-tech plane is expected to arrive, offering the last faint glimmer of hope.

CHAPTER SEVEN
THE BOAT

Juliane's watch stops, leaving her without hours, minutes, or seconds. Time dissolves, and the days blend together, measured only by the rising and setting of the sun. Her sense of hunger abates, but she is slowly starving. Her arms and legs burn with fatigue. All motion becomes burdensome. She floats most of the day in the center of the river, swimming very little.

She cannot see her feet or legs as she moves, but she is not anxious. The caimans' behavior is predictable. She knows that flesh-eating piranhas are dangerous only in shallow, standing water, closer to the shore. And when she leaves the river, she always probes the banks carefully for stingrays.

PIRANHAS

A freshwater fish that dwells in South American rivers and lakes, the piranha is a fierce predator. It can smell blood in water from two miles away. The piranha is often identified by its specialized teeth, a single row of very sharp, tightly packed, triangular-shaped, bladelike teeth in both jaws. The teeth enable it to quickly puncture and shear the flesh of prey. Most piranhas are between five and fifteen inches long, but some can be as long as twenty-five inches.

The piranha has one of the strongest, most forceful bites found in bony fish. Its large jaw muscles coupled with its sharp, jagged teeth enable its mouth to close down and quickly tear flesh from bone. A school of piranhas, which can include more than one hundred individuals, will converge on and devour prey in a feeding frenzy. But though piranhas lurk in vegetation to ambush prey and feed in ravenous, efficient groups, autopsies have shown that they also eat plant food, scales of other fish, seeds, and fruits. However, a shoal of piranhas (between three hundred and five hundred) could devour an adult human in five minutes.

Piranhas dig pits for their eggs during breeding and then circle the pits to protect the newly hatched young. In a dry season, when water is low and food scarce, the piranhas may pose a threat to humans, but they are more likely to feed on a found carcass. As noted, they can quickly strip a drowned mammal down to its bony white skeleton. But they travel in schools not necessarily for attack, but also for protection. Piranhas have natural predators like river dolphins, caimans, and some birds.

Hunger makes piranhas more aggressive, but in captivity they sometimes show anxiety and retreat, even during feeding time. So the piranha is, like many species, the recipient of excited human reports that emphasize its most shock-worthy characteristics.

Still, Juliane was wise to avoid them in her long travail along the water.

Her eyes trail passively over the jungle walls slipping by. Her mind is empty of thoughts. It's too hard to think. Occasionally she clutches a large branch or struggles through knots of floating logs. The nights bring little sleep. Juliane buries her head in her arms and waits for the dawn in a trancelike state. It's ten days since the crash.

In late afternoon of the next day, she crawls onto a sandbank, barely able to make it out of the water. She's worried she might drown if she doesn't rest. Her head nods and sleep promises to untangle her weariness. She blinks, her lids fluttering. Then her eyes open suddenly and widen. Something is right next to her, blended into the light brown water.

A boat.

A canoe bobs gently, the water lapping softly at its sides. Juliane stumbles and splashes to the boat, grasps the bow, and squeezes the wood. *This is not a hallucination. I haven't lost my mind. But where are the people?* A pole and paddles rest on the seats. *I can paddle this boat and get help.*

THE BOAT

This can save me. And then she cuts the thought off. *I can't take this. Someone might need it.* Taking the boat and abandoning people in the wilderness without transportation is unthinkable to Juliane. It was a lesson her parents had drilled into her: In the jungle, people must support and care for one another. If she took the boat, she could leave them stranded, potentially leading to their deaths.

But there's a boat tied here. There must be people.

Juliane turns in a slow circle, scanning for signs of life. No one else is on the river. Her eyes then fall on a crude mud stairway carved by footprints. It winds up the embankment. *How did I not see this? How did I not see the boat before? It was right in front of me.*

Her legs wobble to the first step. Her foot lifts to scale the path, and then she collapses in a heap. Rain-polished foot indentations rise at eye level to the embankment above. She crawls on her hands and knees up the crude stairway. It takes minutes of straining and heaving to scale even one step. Her fingers sink into the earth, and the mud trembles and slides underneath her. *I'm so tired. I'm not in the water now. It's so hard to move. I just want to rest.*

Midway up the nine-foot-high mud stairway, she sees something above her. Surrounded by waving reeds and giant cane plants, the fringe of a palm-thatched roof peeks out. A hut. She pushes up the rest of the bank, steadies herself on her feet, and walks inside. The walls and floor are cut from pona palm wood and styled in the

FOLLOW THE WATER

fashion used by the local Asháninka tribes, with a wood plank floor, poles, and layered palm fronds on a wooden frame roof. The style is like her home at Panguana.

Ropes and tarps hang neatly on hooks, and the general tidiness of the room gives her the sense that someone has recently been there. But there is no warm firepit or other signs of life. In the center of the room sits an outboard motor covered with a plastic tarp. *It's a forty-horsepower engine and here's gasoline. Somebody's nearby. This can is brand-new, and the boat looks new too.* No humans appear, but she sees a narrow path leading into the forest. No voices answer her calls.

Juliane eyes the gasoline can.

A year earlier, her dog Lobo suffered from a fly larvae infestation in a small cut on his neck. The wormlike creatures burrowed under his skin and traveled down to his paw. It wasn't until the dog started limping and smelling of rotting flesh that Juliane's father realized maggots had dug a deep furrow into the dog's leg. The wound swelled and reeked with infection. "We can't use alcohol to help Lobo," her father explained. "The dog will suffer and go crazy with the pain. We have to use kerosene. It doesn't burn flesh as much." They poured the fuel on the wound to drive the maggots to the surface, and then scraped them out when they squirmed to the lip of the wound to breathe. The kerosene saved the dog's leg.

A throbbing pain in Juliane's arm reminds her of

THE BOAT

the maggots in her flesh. Their wobbling, white bodies burst through the wound, writhing and squirming at the surface and beneath her skin. She can see that they have doubled in size. The gas can is not rusted, but her fingers are so weak she can barely twist the top open. She sticks a small hose she finds next to the can into the opening and sucks some gas up into the tube. A small amount of gas won't be missed, and there's plenty left for the owners to run the outboard motor. Holding her finger over the end of the tube, she lays the open end on her shoulder and trickles gas into the wound.

The pain is instant and excruciating. Rather than fleeing out of her body, the maggots first dig deeper into the flesh, biting down on Juliane's muscle. A few more applications chase the desperate, smothered maggots to the surface. She picks them out one by one—thirty half-inch-long maggots in total. Still more nestle in the wound, but she's proud of the accomplishment.

Twilight settles over the hut, and still no one appears. The wooden planks on the floor dig into her elbow, shoulder, and hip. Sleep evades her. A roof covers her head for the first time in eleven days, but a rough, roaring croaking keeps her from sleeping.

Frogs.

Dozens of Peruvian poison dart frogs busy themselves outside and inside of the hut. Hopping, singing, listening. They jump on the boat engine, around

FOLLOW THE WATER

the poles of the hut, in the grasses outside. They move around her body and across the floor.

Her thoughts cloud with fatigue. She stares at the deadly green amphibians. *Can I eat these? Is this my food?* She knows these particular poison dart frogs carry a milder dose of neurotoxin than their brighter, more colorful, and deadly relatives. But they are still filled with chemicals that could paralyze her lungs if the dose is strong enough. *But can't I eat just one?*

She reaches across the floor. *I think I'm starving to death.*

The frog jumps skillfully away.

I don't feel hungry now, but I must eat.

Two shiny green-brown eyes stare at her nose. She moves...and grabs air.

Will just one kill me?

They hop inches from her fingers, too nimble and agile for her feeble attempts to catch them.

PERUVIAN POISON DART FROGS

When an animal has an extremely loud color, it often means that it is deadly. A bright appearance transmits a clear warning to predators that this creature doesn't need to hide; instead, it has a stinger, bite, or poison that can cause harm.

Peruvian poison dart frogs have two horizontal, jaunty neon-green stripes on a dark green body. The frogs produce a neurotoxin that they store in glands under their skin. If this frog is licked or eaten by an animal, pain shoots throughout the animal's body and the poison destroys its nerve cells.

Individual species of poison dart frogs vary in their toxicity, with some carrying enough poison to kill ten adult men. Indigenous Amazonian people have known about the deadly amphibians for thousands of years. Some hunters cover the tips of their arrows and blow darts with the frogs' poison. If a shot pierces the skin and gets into the bloodstream, the prey can drop dead in less than a minute.

Interestingly, these little frogs are not poisonous when raised in captivity. Scientists speculate that the poisonous ants they eat in the rainforest introduce the toxins into their bodies. Most captive poison dart frogs are fed flightless fruit flies or crickets. Without their rainforest diet, they become harmless.

What would have happened if Juliane had eaten one? The Peruvian poison dart frog does carry a smaller amount of toxic chemicals than its more brightly colored cousins, and just one frog would not have killed Juliane. But it would have caused her stomach cramping and nerve pain. If she had eaten more than one, in her emaciated, weakened state, she would have been in danger of dying. She was fortunate she could not catch any.

Juliane's starving body aches on the hard floor. She gets up, drags a tarp from the floor of the hut, and

FOLLOW THE WATER

wobbles outside. The mud is soft, and for the first time in more than a week, she has something manmade to cover her body. The mosquitoes and gnats can't get to her tonight. She slumps to the ground and slips into deep sleep as twilight wanes and night falls.

In the morning Juliane debates taking the boat again. Sluggish thoughts repeat through her head. *Shouldn't I keep moving? Can I take it? The owner could be somewhere in the jungle. He'll need his boat. I can't save my life and threaten others'.* She lies on the riverbank throughout the morning, turning the same thoughts over and over. *Can I even get to the boat and paddle it? I'm so tired and weak.*

Around midday a torrential rainstorm begins. She crawls back into the hut and wraps the tarp around her shoulders. *I know there are shelters in the jungle like this one. Woodcutters near Panguana work deep in the forest and use these huts for emergency shelter. Someone might come.*

Deep in the afternoon, the rain stops. Juliane tells herself to get up and move. Her body doesn't respond. She sits on the palm wood floor, unable to struggle to her feet. Her emotions seesaw. Despair tugs at her. She feels she has simply disappeared from the world. *I think I might die here, and no one will ever know what became of me. The others must have been found long ago. Maybe my mother is with them.* Resolve then fills her. *I'll just rest here another day. Tomorrow I'll go on.* Her thoughts soar with joyful hope—*My mother must already be back home!*—and

THE BOAT

plunge to resignation—*I've gone too long without eating anything. I'm starving. Why come so far only to die in this hut?*

The frogs hop away from her weak, grasping fingers.

Juliane adjusts the tarp around her shoulders. She fades into a stupor and soon feels nothing.

No emotions.

No thoughts.

Twilight shadows fall across the small open hut. Juliane nods off.

Voices of talking men filter into her mind, and then she is awake. *Did I imagine that? Is it like the village I saw? Are they human voices?* Juliane rolls over and looks out the door in the direction of the sound. Three men dressed in loose shirts, pants, and straw hats and carrying machetes emerge from the jungle. They stop when they see her. Fear and surprise cross their straight, even features.

She realizes what she must look like to them. She is rail thin. Her skin is flaming red, bloodied, and blistered. Inflamed bites, mud, and scratches cover her arms, legs, and face. Her ripped dress with its patchwork colors now hangs loosely on her bones. Her hair is a flat cap on her head. Her eyes are still slightly swollen.

What she can't know is that her eyeballs are completely red, even the irises. The damage from the change in pressure when the plane broke apart has not healed.

Her vision isn't affected, but her eyes look like two empty sockets.

The men recoil, on the verge of running. Juliane instinctively knows she has to reassure them. "I'm a girl who was in the LANSA crash. My name is Juliane," she says in Spanish.

The men step closer. Their eyes are wide. They know about the crash and gape at this young girl who has survived almost two weeks in the jungle on her own. Fear of her appearance transforms into concern. This is a young girl desperately in need of help.

The thickets near the hut rustle, and two more soaked men step under the thatched roof. They too freeze in surprise.

The five men—Beltrán Paredes, Carlos Vásquez, Nestor Amasifuén, Marcio Rivera, and Amado Pereira—assure Juliane that they will help her. They then huddle among themselves to discuss. Juliane looks up at them, her small round face filled with relief. But the men are not relaxed, and they debate what to do next. They think she could die tonight. Her head can hardly rise from her emaciated body, and she is in a half stupor. The red, bleeding skin alarms them. She might have internal injuries. How to safely navigate the river at night and get her to help?

The creeping darkness and Juliane's slumped frame convince them to care for her now, in the hut, and then

THE BOAT

set off first thing in the morning. Two of the men will use the outboard motor and boat to ferry her down the river to the nearest town.

Strong, experienced hands set to work. The men light a fire and feed her *fariña*, a roasted, sugary mixture of the local manioc root. The woodcutters thrive on this starchy food while they work in the jungle, but she can manage only a few spoonfuls. The men know not to overfeed her with her shrunken stomach. Too much food at once could kill her. One of them gives Juliane an extra pair of pants and a shirt from his pack to put on. The men respectfully turn their backs as she changes.

REFEEDING SYNDROME—A HIDDEN DANGER OF STARVATION

After days or weeks without food, eating too much too quickly can be deadly. This condition, called refeeding syndrome, happens because a starving body runs low on important nutrients. When food suddenly returns, the body struggles to handle it, causing dangerous shifts in fluids and electrolytes. In severe cases, it can lead to heart failure, seizures, or even death.

History offers a tragic example: A young boy from the Donner Party, stranded in the Sierra Nevada during the brutal winter of 1846, didn't die from starvation alone—but from his body's inability to process food once it finally became available.

Juliane, weak and starving in the jungle, faced the same risk. If she had eaten too much too fast after being rescued, her body might have shut down. Instead, she had to start with small amounts of food, giving her system time to adjust and recover.

The fire casts a warm yellow glow on the small group. The woodcutters clean her cuts and abrasions. The puncture on her arm commands careful attention. The men are impressed that she used the gas to attack the maggots. More gasoline is trickled into the hole in her arm, and one by one, more maggots are carefully teased out with a knife.

The woodcutters don't press her too hard for details, and Juliane tells her story in fits and starts and answers their gentle questions. The men tell her about the search efforts and how all Peru is looking for the airplane.

One of the men smiles. "We thought you were the goddess Yacumama," he says in Spanish. "She lives in the rivers and sucks up humans. She's shaped like a snake with a long white body. It was your empty eyes and white hair. And there is no one else here for miles. Especially not whites," he adds. "It's a good thing you spoke right away to us. We were going to run." The men chuckle.

YACUMAMA AND *EL TUNCHE*

Mischievous and deadly spirits lurk throughout the Amazon, in the minds of people. Deep sounds in the rainforest night and half-glimpsed animal forms become mythical creatures that are blamed for everything bad that happens and even threaten to swallow people whole.

Yacumama is a nature goddess who lives in the water. She can burst furiously to the surface with gleaming eyes and suck up any person who dares to come near her. The Yacumama tale is traced back to the Incan civilization and sightings of the anaconda snake, but many cultures around the world have fictitious stories of dangerous and powerful water creatures.

The whistle of *el tunche* panics and terrifies people in both the Peruvian rainforest and cities. Its high-pitched whistles are attached to legends of memory loss, insanity, and death. Scary stories about *el tunche* have terrified children for generations, including a very young Juliane.

The cause of all this trouble is *Tunchiornis ochraceiceps ferrugineifrons*, or the tawny-crowned greenlet. This small yellow-gray member of the cuckoo family has a puff of rusty orange feathers as a crown and forages in clearings in the rainforest, often in areas cleared out by leaf-cutter ants. The call of *el tunche* is long and mournful and does sound like a human whistle.

FOLLOW THE WATER

Juliane realizes the truth: They are on a river that is uninhabited, and finding these woodcutters was simply amazing luck. These men work hundreds of miles of forest on their own, using the river as their only entry and exit point. If she had missed them, she would have continued to wander, floating in the bends of the river until she died. No one would ever have found her.

As it was, the woodcutters almost didn't come to the hut on this day. Only the intense rainstorms pushed them back to their shelter.

Revived by the sugary manioc root, Juliane feels a warm energy flow into her. The concerned faces, grizzled beards, and gentle lines around the men's eyes come into clearer focus. She asks, "What about the other passengers? Are they already rescued?"

The men fall silent. They look away from her and exchange glances. One finally returns her gaze and answers in a low, hoarse voice. "No, *señorita*. Not even the plane has been found yet. It has simply disappeared, as if the jungle closed its fist around it. As far as we know, you are the only survivor."

Juliane draws in a deep breath. It seems impossible that she can be the only survivor. *There were so many people on the plane. The boys I talked to. The families. They could have escaped like me. The only survivor? Me? If I'm the only one, then...* And with a heavy dread she realizes what this means.

THE BOAT

She asks. "My mother isn't found?"

The men stare silently, until one speaks quietly. "No one."

Juliane can't find the words to ask more questions.

The group settles down in the hut. She secretly wishes that she could creep out onto the soft riverbank, away from the hard planks of the hut floor. The men cover her with their only mosquito net and feed her some more food. The insect sounds of the night swell, and she drifts to sleep to the sound of hushed Spanish conversation. The men soon lie down to sleep as well, encircling her like the spokes on a wheel.

In the early-morning darkness, the group walks to the embankment. Oddly, now that she's had some food and knows she's saved, her wounds hurt terribly. Two of the men carry her down the embankment and lay her gently on the boat's deck. They cover her with a tarp and get in with her.

Her body surrenders. Utter and complete exhaustion consumes her. She trusts her fate to her rescuers. She watches the river flow and the jungle glide by. She dozes and then rouses to talk to the men. At first there are no people on the shore, and the men must navigate carefully around floating debris. Hours into the journey, the river joins a large tributary. Logs, palm fronds, and plant matter clear out of the current. One boat, and then more, appear, dotting the brown water. Other river passengers transporting livestock, harvests, and people wave at her boat. Her eyes drink in smiling faces and the goodwill of the people. They call out greetings. When they notice Juliane, they look at her with curiosity but say nothing. Juliane's physical weakness can't suppress her soaring feelings of relief. *This is not a dream. I'm going home. It's true.*

The woodcutters continue to give her small amounts of food and water. At noon, the men reach a small clearing and stop to eat at a house they know. A woman and children rush out to greet them but stop when they see Juliane. The woman begins a terrified cry. "Those eyes! Those terrible eyes. I can't look at them." The children run away screaming.

The trio continue down the river. At times she finds herself watching her rescuers' faces. These are the kindest of men. They have saved her life. Sleep overtakes her.

CHAPTER EIGHT
AT LAST

After eleven hours on the river, the woodcutters' long boat eases up to a small wooden dock in a town called Tournavista. Two men gently lift Juliane to shore. She meets their eyes with warm gratitude. Two villagers suddenly appear with a stretcher. She insists on trying to walk, and several people prop her up and guide her into a house. They drape a clean blanket over her shoulders. Out of nowhere, someone rushes up and takes a photo.

The village explodes with excitement at her arrival. People spill out of the houses to see who has been rescued. A shortwave radio operator broadcasts the miraculous news of Juliane's appearance, and the news shoots throughout the country. In Pucallpa, more than fifty miles away, families swarm into the central plaza. Hope and joy surge as they hug, laugh, and cry at the incredible news. *Can this be possible? Are there more survivors? Could my child be alive? My wife? My husband?*

A nurse appears in the house. She gently examines Juliane and then cleans and bandages her open wounds. The leg slash is now red and swelling. She readies a penicillin shot to fight the infection.

Alarmed, Juliane draws back. "No, no, my father is allergic. This could kill me."

The nurse knows a penicillin allergy is not inherited, but she understands the young girl's anxiety. After all she's been through, one missed penicillin shot won't matter. She gives her another type of antibacterial injection.

A famous American pilot, Jerrie Cobb, is in Tournavista. She volunteers to fly Juliane to Yarinacocha, a small settlement in the jungle where missionaries are studying Indigenous languages. There are doctors there who can immediately treat her injuries.

Cobb's small bush plane is a workhorse, a cargo hauler with two seats up front and empty space for boxes, supplies, and luggage in the back. Juliane eyes it warily but is too weak to protest. Fear washes over her as the pilot

AT LAST

places her in a makeshift bed on the floor and smiles. She tries to reassure Juliane of her skill. "Don't worry. I was one of the first women to be trained as an astronaut in the United States," Cobb says.

The announcement of this achievement does little to quell Juliane's terror at the idea of flying again. The little plane vibrates and shakes as it rattles down the runway. The twenty-minute flight and deep banking turns terrify her, and Cobb's reassurance that she's as safe as if she "were in the arms of an angel" barely registers.

JERRIE COBB

The bold pilot who frightened Juliane with her deep turns was a groundbreaking aviator. Her father taught her to fly, and at the age of sixteen she was barnstorming over the Great Plains, dropping advertisements.

Flying was in her bones. At seventeen, she had her commercial pilot's license and began to work delivering military planes around the world. She went on to become, in her twenties, one of the first executives in the airline industry and broke many speed, altitude, and distance records.

In 1959, Cobb was part of Mercury 13, a group of elite female pilots who underwent the physical and psychological exams to become astronauts for NASA. The women endured grueling physical endurance and medical tests, including submerging their feet in ice water, having cold water shot into their ears, and drinking castor oil. Cobb aced the gyroscope test, where a candidate was enclosed in a giant metal box and then spun in three directions at once. To pass, the pilots could not panic or get sick as they worked to bring the machine under control.

Cobb scored in the top 2 percent of all test subjects, men and women, but NASA failed to break free from the sexism of the 1960s. No female pilot was selected to join the elite astronaut corps. In fact, then–Vice President Lyndon Johnson lobbied against the addition of women to the space program.

This was a bitter disappointment for Cobb. She spent several years asking Congress to revive the project, but was not successful. By 1963, she'd decided to buy her own plane and fly to the Amazon basin. Intent on combining her flying skills with humanitarian efforts, Cobb joined the ranks of bush pilots, logging tens of thousands of hours. She flew over endless stretches of the Andes and the Amazon rainforest to deliver medicine, food, and supplies to Indigenous populations. She was nominated for the Nobel Peace Prize for her humanitarian efforts.

In 1978, NASA opened the astronaut application to everyone, regardless of race or gender. As of 2025, one hundred women have flown into space.

After the plane finally lands at the missionary settlement, Juliane is tucked into a bed in the family home of Dr. Frank Lindholm, who is puzzled that Juliane's injuries do not match the violence of the crash. How she avoided more catastrophic lacerations, bone breaks, or internal injuries as she endured the plane's destruction, a two-mile fall to the earth, and then eleven days in the Amazon can only be described as phenomenal.

AT LAST

Although Juliane felt little pain as she pushed through the wilderness, the treatment of her wounds is excruciatingly painful. Dr. Lindholm tears off a twenty-inch length of gauze, dips it in an iodine solution, and packs her arm and leg wounds. He pushes the dressings deep into her lesions to quell infection. She endures the searing pain, clenching her teeth to keep from screaming. Afterward, she bathes and eats her first real meal in almost two weeks—a chicken sandwich. Safe, fed, and surrounded by the warmth of the Lindholm family, she easily falls asleep in a soft bed and between clean sheets.

Air Force Commander del Carpio holds a press conference in Pucallpa to confirm Juliane's rescue. A volcano burst of reporters has again descended on the town, hunting for more information. Del Carpio orders an embargo on any contact with Juliane from the press corps or outsiders. He reports that her injuries are mild. This sends another jolt of euphoric hope through the families waiting for news. *If this young person made it, why couldn't mine?*

The woodcutters Marcio Rivera and Amado Pereira relate Juliane's descriptions of the smaller stream leading to a larger one and the broad clump of nearly impenetrable *caña brava*. The local rainforest workers know the spot and give Commander del Carpio's team specific directions on how to get there.

Pilots take off to search the area for the plane.

FOLLOW THE WATER

They plan to drop packets of food and water in hopes that there are more survivors. It is not possible to land a plane in the area, and the teams must hike in or rappel from helicopters once the plane is found. It will take careful planning to stage a rescue. The hopes of dozens of families ride with them.

On the morning of January 5, twelve days after the plane crash and the day after she fell asleep at the Lindholms', Juliane opens her eyes and peers around. It takes her a moment to adjust and realize where she is. *I'm here. I'm with the living. I'm back.* But no joy swells through her. Her thoughts are factual. Her mind steers away from emotion and entertains no thoughts of the future.

As she lies on the bed, the door opens and her father steps into the room. His thinning hair and deep-set eyes convey total exhaustion.

"How are you doing?" he asks.

Juliane answers in a small voice. "Good."

Her father sits on the bed, and they fall into each other's arms. Afterward, the pair look at each other but say little. She knows this should be a moment of relief, that she is safe. He is here to take care of her. But she remains numb, with no sense of her emotions. She knows she feels happiness and love in her father's presence, but they are not coursing through her heart or head. She and her father sit in silence. Finally, he asks about her mother.

Juliane tells her father every detail—the Andes,

AT LAST

the storm, the lightning strike, the fall, and the journey through the rainforest. She watches his face crumple in disappointment when he realizes that she never saw Maria again after the accident. Hans's reaction does not crush her; in fact, she feels a sense of apathy, and of being cut off from her feelings.

For Hans, the joy of Juliane's return is laced with sorrow. He realizes he will never see Maria alive again.

As if a light switch has been flipped, Juliane's body finally responds to her wounds and injuries. Her temperature soars, and Dr. Lindholm fights to lower it. A few days after the fever came, it just as quickly disappears.

Her left knee swells to the size of a softball. An X-ray reveals a torn ligament. Dr. Lindholm is stunned that she was able to walk and swim for eleven days, let alone not feel any pain in that knee, or from any of her other injuries.

Juliane most likely produced more adrenaline than usual as she struggled through the rainforest. Adrenaline is a hormone released in the body when someone has extreme emotions and physical stress. The chemical causes the person to have more energy and helps to block pain.

In all, she suffered from a bruised spinal cord, a broken collarbone, a torn ACL, a partially fractured shin, a strained neck vertebra, several deep cuts on her arms and legs, a second-degree sunburn, burst blood vessels

FOLLOW THE WATER

in her eyes, and hundreds of insect bites, including the maggots in her arm. Her injuries were serious but could have been much graver, given all that she went through.

Based on Juliane's description of her journey and the woodcutters' guidance, planes conduct an aerial search of the *caña brava* area and finally find the wreckage of the plane. The fuselage and the debris of the crash are scattered over a huge section of the jungle. Since it's impossible to land a plane in the area, military search parties and desperate family members set off on foot to the crash area. They struggle to break through twelve miles of intense plant growth to reach the impact site. Torrential rains, hilly terrain, and ankle-deep mud make progress grueling.

Before the ground crew can reach the site, another group in a helicopter finds the wreck, and rescue workers rappel to the ground. Later the same day, the ground crew arrives at the site, and the two teams work together to clear a helicopter landing pad.

The next morning, the rescue teams find the plane's tail, and the reality of their mission sinks in. Bodies are discovered cast about in a two-square-mile area. Some of the people are suspended in the trees. Clothes, suitcases, presents, and food litter the ground, but there are no other signs of life. The rescue turns into a recovery operation.

Juliane is the sole survivor.

AT LAST

Reporters figure out where Juliane is and pile into the religious community. Commander del Carpio continues to prevent the Peruvian press from speaking with Juliane. He places a guard on Juliane's door, and her father shoos most other journalists away. The stories the newspapers publish are based on secondhand information or are just made up. Sensitivity is forgotten, and one report describes how she has no tears for her mother but cries bitterly when she learns of a pet bird's death.

Hans decides to let only the German magazine *Stern* interview her, in hopes that it will help settle down the press. For several days she gives interviews to *Stern* and details everything she knows. Her father attends all the interviews and afterward sits quietly in a corner of Juliane's room. He speaks rarely and his face is a blank mask. He is in a world of deep sorrow.

After a makeshift morgue is constructed in Pucallpa, Hans flies there, searching for his wife. It's now five days since Juliane emerged from the jungle. She rests and gains strength at the missionary station but is plagued by guilt. *Why didn't I skip the dance after graduation and come home that day? We wouldn't have been on the plane. Why did I want so badly to participate in the celebration? Why didn't my mother survive?* She knows these are also her father's thoughts. During one intense moment he blurts out, "Why did you have to take the LANSA flight?" But they do not speak about it further. Juliane appreciates that her father is a man of few words, but communication about the accident, and their emotions and feelings, are sealing off.

On the afternoon of January 12, her father returns from Pucallpa, pale but composed. He found Maria and was able to identify her. He tells Juliane that her mother is dead.

Juliane's and his sorrows are compounded by a terrible revelation: Her mother's body was found farther from the other victims and had barely decomposed. The Koepckes know that any mammal that dies in the jungle is quickly set upon by scavengers and bacteria, so the body immediately starts to decompose. The corpses showed that at least six passengers, including Maria, may have survived the crash. They were not acutely deteriorated. She appeared to have broken her pelvis and may have lain alive for days waiting for rescue. Severe injuries prevented the other passengers from walking, and they too died days after the crash, waiting for help.

Juliane and her father do not discuss this devastating news. Hans had clashed several times with the search leaders, believing that they were not acting quickly and diligently enough. He thinks that his wife might have survived if only they had tried harder to find her. The idea tortures him. In the months after the crash, they'll both bury the grief deep inside them. Juliane stays at

AT LAST

the missionary station for the time being, and then with friends to avoid the maelstrom of public interest in her. Her father remains nearby, often sitting quietly in her room staring into space. The doctors continue her medical treatment, and she preoccupies herself with friendly visits and letter writing as she prepares to return to Panguana.

CHAPTER NINE
A DIFFERENT KIND OF STORM

After four weeks, Juliane returns home. The familiar jungle at Panguana gives her peace. She is reunited with her beloved Lobo, and she cares for her pet animals. Once again, she awakens in her own bed, surrounded by familiar rooms and the forest she loves.

Her father remains distant. He has been Juliane's teacher, friend, and mentor, as well as her father, but losing his life partner devastates him and leaves him remote and emotionally shut down. He continues his scientific work as he grapples with how to proceed without Maria. He does not share his thoughts or feelings with Juliane.

For Juliane, the loss of her mother seems unreal. At

times it feels as if her mother is on a work trip and might come home at any moment. Grief seems to have left her as well. She thinks of Maria's death as a theory. Much later she learns the difference between understanding something and grasping it.

She anticipates her return to Lima so she can begin to study for the *Arbitur*, the entrance exams for universities in Germany. She recalls how she and her mother had already discussed that she would study biology and go to school in Germany. It'll take two years of intensive study to ready her for the European system, and she relishes the idea that she'll be in Lima studying and surrounded by friends. Life will return to almost normal.

On several occasions reporters find their way to Panguana. Peruvian and international papers, television, and radio clamor for more information about the girl who survived an unbelievable crash and walked out of the jungle. An investigation into the cause of the crash has not begun, and officials are still not releasing further information. The journalists are hungry for more to the story. Juliane's father protects her and chases them away.

Five weeks pass quickly in Panguana, and Juliane returns to Lima with dreams of normalcy. But while recuperating in Panguana, she became an international hero—the girl who miraculously survived both the crash and the perils of the Amazon. Hiding from

FOLLOW THE WATER

curiosity seekers and the press is impossible. All Peru and the world want to learn about Juliane and how she walked out of the jungle.

She stands out in a crowd because of her light blonde hair, and she is instantly recognized because of all the press coverage. Strangers come up to her in the street and ask her questions. People reach out to touch her, hug her, or ask for an autograph. She follows her father's instruction and grants no more interviews. Reporters hound her everywhere and pepper her with questions on the street. A troop of paparazzi camp outside her door, waiting to pounce. They use telephoto lenses and try to take pictures through her windows. She cannot leave the house without being besieged.

She is a young, attractive girl who accomplished what grown, trained men fail to do. She survived both a plane crash and the trek home. Everyone wants to know more. How did she do it? What went through her mind? How does she feel now?

The papers and television run and rerun recycled photos and stories riddled with errors and outright lies. In a devastating twist, some journalists accuse Juliane of abandoning other crash survivors, claiming she thought only of herself. They write that she left the injured behind in her desperate bid to escape the green hell, that survivors were wandering the forest, begging and crying out for help, while she ran away from them.

A DIFFERENT KIND OF STORM

On a hot April day, Juliane agrees to go swimming at a country club with a girlfriend. A stealthy group of television reporters sneak into the club and surround the girls. Her friend suggests that if she gives an interview, they might leave her alone. Juliane decides to give her only interview since the *Stern* article. Seated on a swing in a bikini, she cheerfully answers questions, hoping the reporters soon leave. After a while the same old questions end, and the cameras and notepads depart. The girls enjoy the afternoon.

Hans is furious when he sees the interview on television. Her smiling answers informing the world that she's doing just fine enrage him. He yells at Juliane. *So that's how you mourn your mother!* And so with no warning he announces that she is to return to Germany immediately, to live with her aunt and grandmother and pursue her studies. No amount of pleading or arguments can change his mind.

At seventeen, Juliane is not in charge of her own choices. Their privacy in Peru is gone, and Hans's deep sorrow and anger at the loss of Maria drive his decision. He is unable to connect with Juliane. She is also a painful reminder. Juliane looks like her mother and has the same curious, positive demeanor. And tragically for both, Maria didn't survive the crash.

FOLLOW THE WATER

Within a few weeks Hans Koepcke places Juliane on a flight to travel alone to Kiel, Germany, a port city on the Baltic Sea. Her fear of flying is overwhelmed by her emotions. She spends most of the long flight lost in thoughts about the life she's leaving and what awaits her.

Germany, a country she has visited in the past and liked, is the polar opposite of her home. There are no steamy, tropical rainforests; broad, flat, mocha-colored rivers; or monkeys or other jungle wildlife. Snowy, cold European winters, crowded cities, and wildlands filled with coniferous forests wait for her. Her childhood is over. Her mother is gone. She doesn't know it at the time, but she will never return to Panguana with her father.

Life in Germany means new friends and preparing for university. Juliane lives in a cozy apartment with her father's sister, Cordula, and her grandmother. But she soon understands that she is still not completely well. Her skin and the whites of her eyes have taken on a deep yellow color. Tests reveal that she has a severe case of hepatitis, a dangerous inflammation of the liver. She most likely picked up a virus from the water she drank in the jungle to survive. Her anticipated start to her new life is stalled, and she spends time in the hospital and

A DIFFERENT KIND OF STORM

then weeks resting in her new home. Finally, months after her arrival, she begins school in Kiel.

As Juliane settles into life in Germany, she shows little feeling about the tragedy. New friends treat her kindly and she spends a joyful time getting to know her extended family, but she doesn't speak much about her ordeal, recovery, or her mother.

During the day, she seems numbed to her memories and emotions about the crash. At night her subconscious brings nightmares of roaring engines and a feeling of hurtling fast through the air. She also dreams of her mother. The dreams evaporate in the morning light. The cocoon of studies and school life shelters her from publicity, and she avoids most contact with reporters and curiosity seekers. There is little time to think about what has happened.

Two years after she arrives in Germany, she finishes preparing for the university and passes all her exams. She then enters the Christian-Albrechts University in Kiel, the school her mother also attended, where she will earn a bachelor of science.

By choosing science, she will be able to explore the mysteries of nature and feed her natural curiosity. Ever since leaving her home in Panguana, she's nursed the need to return. She's sure that her studies will give her the opportunity to go home to Peru. But in the meantime, her days are filled with studying and classes.

Unknown to Juliane at the time, she is most likely suffering from post-traumatic stress disorder (PTSD). This condition develops in some people when a devastating event occurs in their life, typically involving violence or other physical or emotional trauma.

In the 1970s, little was known about PTSD. Now researchers understand that about one in three who experience severe trauma develop the syndrome. Brain scans reveal that a PTSD sufferer's hippocampus appears smaller in size. This area is responsible for memory and emotions.

One symptom of PTSD is nightmares. Another is emotional numbing. Juliane's initial lack of emotion in the early days after the crash may have been a PTSD symptom. At the time, doctors did not know that the tragic accident had left deep mental as well as physical scars that could last for years.

Friends and especially her aunt comforted her and gave her support from the moment she arrived in Germany, but like her body, her mind needed time to heal. Ideally, she would have had counseling and ongoing support to handle her symptoms. Supervised psychological care helps survivors navigate back into the world. She had none of this guidance.

It's not until three years after she arrives in Germany that the permanence of the loss of her mother hits her. It's the Christmas season. Thoughts of her mother lead to tears. Tears lead to days of uncontrollable crying. All her defenses evaporate, and a delayed grief and sense of loss sweep over her. She mourns deeply for her mother. But this remains her personal and private expression of grief. She and her father will seldom discuss Maria's death or the impact of her loss on the family.

In 1975, her father returns to Germany. He becomes a professor at the university in Hamburg, leaving Panguana in the care of their family friend Moro. Hans and Juliane visit each other frequently, and she attends scientific conferences with him. During the next few years, Hans mentors many students who travel to Panguana to study. Moro assists the researchers and manages the research station in Panguana. He and Hans communicate by mail.

From Hamburg, Hans teaches, writes, and speaks to secure Panguana's future. The small patch of land that was their home has a unique biodiversity. It is an ecological hot spot. These are areas of the earth that are threatened by human habitation and misuse.

Many species found in Panguana are endemic, or not known anywhere else, and the animal and plant concentration is unusually high. The genetic diversity in the region is further enhanced because different populations of the same species, which are usually geographically separate, overlap in the Panguana region.

Another key aspect of Panguana's research value is its one-of-a-kind vertical plant-growing zones. Each zone harbors rare plant and animal species found nowhere else on Earth, often belonging to the same families. Two of the least-studied areas are the upper canopy and overstory.

How to reach the heights for meaningful observation puzzled scientists for years. Early researchers employed barbaric methods of data gathering. They would chop down trees and shoot animals. Modern technology gives us more peaceful opportunities to spy on the goings-on high above the ground. Today, sophisticated engineered platforms, cameras, DNA testing, and drones eavesdrop on the high-rise societies.

The idea that Panguana should be preserved and expanded as an ecological hot spot becomes a focus of Hans's work. He envisions ongoing scientific exploration and scientific research from teams around the world. He desires to protect the station from deforestation and stop the development of pasturelands and farms. Gold miners and loggers will be turned away.

Hans still has not returned to Peru and he will not realize his vision. From Germany it is impossible to have the face-to-face contact he needs to negotiate successfully for more land. The Peruvian government and

A DIFFERENT KIND OF STORM

landowners are halfway around the world. Panguana remains a small research station, nestled in a remote area of the Amazon—and surrounded by threats. Illegal traffickers covet it for its timber and gold deposits, and there is talk of a national development project running through that section of the jungle.

CHAPTER TEN
A RETURN HOME

In 1977, Juliane finishes her undergraduate biology work in Germany. She returns to Peru for the first time since the accident to research butterfly wings.

Juliane is excited about the return home. She longs to see her familiar haunts in Lima and her school friends. To her dismay, packs of reporters stalk her in the city. She doesn't shed herself of them until she leaves for Panguana.

When she arrives, she is once again astonished by the beauty and life in the rainforest. The green cosmos is a perfect fit for her curiosity and research. She spends a month happily immersed in studying butterfly wings.

The compound and the surrounding forest have so

A RETURN HOME

far been spared from significant human encroachment. She notices more development in Pucallpa and better-maintained roads. The only event that mars her return to the research station is a sting on her thigh from the powerful bullet ant. After three months in Peru, she returns to Germany to write about her findings for her thesis.

When her thesis is done, she has to pick one topic to study more deeply so she can earn her PhD, the final degree a scientist needs. She decides to study zoology and is accepted into Ludwig Maximilian University of Munich. Juliane is determined to return to Peru to conduct her research and is intent on choosing a creature that is abundant in Panguana, preferably a mammal.

The last thing she considers is bats. They flit around at night and are ugly and creepy. Or are they? It is her father who points out their uniqueness. Bats are the only mammal that can fly. They are nocturnal and hunt at night. They find their way through the air with echolocation. This is how bats fly in the dark, using sound. They make high-pitched noises (often too high for humans to hear), and when the sound waves hit an object—like an insect, a tree, or a wall—they bounce back as echoes. By listening to these echoes, bats learn an object's location, size, and movement. This helps them find food and navigate in total darkness. Juliane is intrigued. She packs her bags for Peru, ready to spend a year and

FOLLOW THE WATER

a half studying and documenting the bat species living in Panguana.

The Koepckes' friend Moro and his family welcome Juliane back. They have built a new home next to Panguana to keep an eye on the area. At the research station, she finds scientists sharing stories of their discoveries and difficulties, much like the days of her youth. Her parents are not here, but their spirit of discovery and love of the forest resonate all around her.

Cook fires burn, and wafts of outdoor meals fill the air. Time off from studies and observation are spent with Moro's family. Neighbors teach her natural healing techniques with jungle plants, and how to slaughter and cook caimans, tapirs, and other animals they hunt in the forest. Feasts with jungle recipes celebrate the good times. These are people who love and respect their forest home and live in harmony with nature.

Out in the field she melds with the jungle, at home and relaxed in the wild. During the day she crawls into hollow tree trunks or under riverbanks to take peaceful naps. Nighttime is bat time. She sets up and checks her bat traps.

Mist nets (rectangular nets made of fine threads) capture her subjects near mineral licks, water, and feeding locations. She learns to extract netted bats from behind and fold back their wings. This helps her avoid their teeth. She enjoys petting the exquisitely soft fur

A RETURN HOME

of captured bats before she weighs them, noting their sex, age, reproductive status, wing size, and many other kinds of body measurements. She then releases them carefully back into their home.

NOT FLYING MICE

Many people harbor negative feelings about bats. Folklore characterizes them as flying at people and getting tangled in their hair. Wicked bats turn into murderous vampires. They bring bad luck. Of course, none of this is true.

While bats look like mice with wings, they are not remotely related to rodents. The jury's still out on bats' closest living relative, but carnivores like dogs are on the list—and so are whales!

There are more than 1,400 kinds of bats around the world, including forty-seven species found in the United States and Canada. In fact, about one out of every five mammals on Earth is a bat! They can live everywhere except extreme polar and desert regions. Ancient bat ancestors have been around for more than fifty million years.

Juliane identified fifty-two bat species in her 1987 publication: "Ecological Studies on a Bat Community in the Tropical

Rainforest of Peru." Since then, five more species have been identified. This speaks to the amazing diversity of life around Panguana.

Bats are one of the most important animals on the planet. These nighttime fliers consume crop-devouring and disease-carrying insects. They pollinate plants like bananas, peaches, and agaves. Fruit-eating bats disperse seeds that help forests grow.

Their night flight is accomplished through echolocation, the ability to make sounds that bounce off objects. The speed at which the sound returns helps bats understand where objects are in the dead of night.

Bat DNA and genes reveal superpowers around health and age. They can repair their damaged DNA and modify their immune systems to fend off viruses and reduce inflammation.

Bats do carry deadly viruses, such as rabies and all kinds of coronaviruses, including COVID-19. Scientists believe human encroachment into bat territory spreads these diseases. Juliane was fully vaccinated for rabies and worked carefully with her subjects.

Bats love company, and different species of bats will roost together in mega colonies. This helps viruses spread between individuals and species. Few bats die from these viruses, but they can spread the disease to humans through physical contact. Therefore, you should never touch any bat you find.

In just a year and a half of studying bats, Juliane catalogs fifty-two species. She chronicles their feeding habits and daily life, counts them in roosts, and spies on their conversations with an ultrasonic "bat detector."

A RETURN HOME

Occasionally, a rare ocelot, a medium-size jungle cat, crosses her path. Once she stumbles onto a jaguar kill, only to be frightened away by a rolling growl from deep in the night shadows. Panguana has some established observation trails, initially fashioned from animal paths. These are used by the scientists, but she leaves the trails to find the bats. She tracks her subjects deep into the night and emerges out of the web of trees and brush in the early hours of the morning. After a bath in the river, some food, and a little reading, she snuffs her candle and falls asleep.

As Juliane works at Panguana, the glory of its enormous complexity and interconnectedness fills her mind and soul. She is now conducting scientific research that is her own. She is not an extension of her parents, but a life spent learning by their sides enriches her days. An expanded awareness of her surroundings quickens in her. She is more aware than ever of the musty smells, humid temperatures, rains, and never-ending grunts, clicks, and tweets of the wildlife.

It is at this time the vow made many years ago on the isolated riverbank reawakens in her mind. *I must be alive for a reason. My life must mean something. If I survive, I will make a difference in the world.* These words return to her, and she now knows she has a task. She will help her father create a permanent nature reserve at Panguana.

CHAPTER ELEVEN
GERMANY

After eighteen months in the rainforest, Juliane heads back to Munich to start the work of processing the massive amount of data she gathered about bat communities. Juliane throws herself into her studies. She enjoys it, and in 1987, her publication about the bats of Panguana is accepted and admired. Juliane's childhood in Panguana gave her a deep knowledge of the Amazon, but becoming a scientist required years of formal education. After more than ten years of study, research, travel, and writing, she becomes Dr. Juliane Koepcke, PhD in zoology. She is thirty-two years old.

Days, months, and then years pass happily for Juliane in Germany. She meets and marries a fellow scientist, Erich Diller, an empathetic listener who makes her laugh. It's the match she needs. She earns a position as the head of the Bavarian State Collection of Zoology in Munich. She is now a working scientist. She makes plans to return to Panguana and work on expanding the research station.

But in the 1990s, events in Peru near Panguana make travel perilous. Armed revolutionaries occupy areas of the rainforest near the research station. Communist guerilla fighters known as the Shining Path attack Indigenous people, white people, reformers, and political opposition throughout the country—anybody who speaks against them or their tactics. During this time almost seventy thousand people are killed or disappear because of the armed conflict.

Juliane and her father monitor the unfolding strife from Germany. They keep in constant contact with the Módena family and other friends in the country. Moro is officially appointed administrator and the Koepckes' local representative.

The guerillas do not attack the people of Panguana, but the area becomes very attractive to gold and timber seekers. Discovering a deep vein of gold could make a person rich. Prospecting pits cut through the pristine Amazon, and the chemicals the miners use for gold extraction pollute the rivers. Likewise, timber harvesters can make small fortunes from cutting large, mature rainforest trees. Moro successfully protects Panguana from timber speculators and illegal gold miners.

Juliane, now Dr. Diller, continues to build her professional life. She writes scientific papers and magazine articles about the beauty and biological importance of Peru and Panguana.

For years she has avoided discussing the crash and refused interviews from the media. After she earned her PhD, the work in Germany and personal life with her husband were her primary focus. The upheaval in Peru keeps her from returning to Panguana. Finally, in 1998, this changes. She will return to Peru. Her inspiration is a phone call from a very unusual man who wants to interview Juliane and make a movie.

CHAPTER TWELVE
HERZOG

The dejected movie crew Juliane and her mother passed by all those years ago in Jorge Chávez International Airport in Lima was led by the award-winning German film director Werner Herzog. He was about to start filming a movie called *Aguirre, the Wrath of God* in the Amazon near the Pachitea River. It was a stroke of luck for Herzog and his crew that they did not get seats on LANSA Flight 508 on that fateful Christmas Eve.

Werner Herzog is tall, athletic, and serious. He is known for feature films and factual documentaries using careful camera techniques to capture emotionally moving portraits of his subjects.

FOLLOW THE WATER

Though it is twenty-seven years after the accident and Juliane avoids discussing the past, Herzog persuades her to return to Peru with him to participate in a documentary about the crash and her struggle in the jungle. She realizes such a film will refocus popular attention on her, but this might also help her protect Panguana and its future. The brutal and extensive violence from the conflict with the Shining Path guerillas is abating. A return to Peru also excites her.

Herzog travels with Juliane from Germany to Lima to Pucallpa, interviewing her every step of the way. In keeping with his standard filming methods, he has no prepared script or list of questions. Through gentle conversation, he prompts Juliane to retrace her route and relive the events. His conversations with her go with the flow. He is more of a poet than a journalist, stretching out feelers and listening carefully, seeking to understand the soul of Juliane.

He arranges for her to be in the same airplane seat by the wing that she occupied on the doomed flight. Once on the ground in Pucallpa, he escorts her to a monument erected in memory of those lost in the crash. Carved in stone is a map of the flight and the trail that Juliane forged to reach safety. A six-foot angel weeps and buries her head in her arm. The smooth white stone has embedded pictures of the deceased and entombs many of the remains of the Peruvians who perished. Juliane has never seen it before. She is struck by how young many of the victims were.

Herzog and Juliane travel to the crash site by helicopter. The overland trip through the rainforest is still dangerous. There are no direct trails or roads to the area of the crash, and all these years later the debris are still scattered over ten miles. Herzog arranges for a team of woodcutters to clear a landing pad by the remains of the plane. Much of the crash must be hacked and cleared of vines and brush by machete. Juliane and Herzog, in rubber boots and bandannas and carrying machetes, retrace her first moments in the rainforest after she fell.

The movie crew locates the seat Juliane clung to during her plunge to the earth and much of the fuselage scattered in pieces on the forest floor. With slow progress the film crew pushes miles through the uninhabited jungle to find the grease-covered engine and propeller that Juliane passed so many years before. Even a quarter of a century later, they find broken suitcases and Christmas wreaths and presents hanging in the trees.

Juliane recounts her battle through the jungle and her days of floating and paddling on the river. Herzog reunites her with the people who helped her. They meet

FOLLOW THE WATER

with Marcio Rivera, one of the woodcutters who first fed and tended to her before ferrying her down the river to Tournavista. Now, so many years later, she has the chance to return the favor.

He had recently been stung by a stingray, and lay dying from infection on a remote Amazon shore. Passing canoeists came by and took him to safety, but only in exchange for his rifle. Herzog later tracked them down and bought the rifle back. In the film, Juliane presents it to him as a gift upon reuniting with her rescuer after many years. She embraces him and vividly recounts for Herzog how the woodcutters rescued her.

Herzog asks probing questions. He pushes her to reveal her feelings but knows when to pull back. The questions do not disturb her. Rather, the effect is the opposite. Juliane answers honestly and factually, like the clear-thinking scientist she is. Part of her also wants to help Herzog with his project by cooperating. She speaks in detail and bravely retells her story.

Since the days of the crash and losing her mother, she has not seen a therapist or spoken to many others about the crash. The work with Werner Herzog allows her to speak openly about her fear, anguish, and pain during the eleven days in the rainforest. She is now ready to lobby and push for the expansion of her rainforest home.

AN INTERESTING MAN

In 1971, European filmmaker Werner Herzog and his crew sat frustrated in Lima's Jorge Chávez Airport, unable to get tickets on LANSA Flight 508. He saw a girl in a miniskirt and flimsy shoes walk past him and board with her mother. He and his crew escaped certain death that day because the plane was full. Herzog would always remember the girl on the doomed flight. He has said that her odyssey through the jungle caught something deep inside him.

Herzog's own trek through life has been filled with adventure. His journey has taken him from a tiny, cold house with no plumbing in a remote Bavarian village to Mexico, Hollywood, Alaska, the Amazon—anywhere there was a captivating story to tell.

Though he grew up in extreme poverty—he did not use a phone until he was seventeen—he developed a love for reading and storytelling. In his youth he had many jobs, including milking cows and lugging milk and beer up mountain trails. As a young man he rode a bucking horse in a Mexican rodeo.

Herzog ended up eating a strange dinner in 1979. He publicly told filmmaker Errol Morris, "I will eat my shoe" if Morris completed a project. Morris did so, and Herzog cooked and ate his shoe.

Another incident testifies to Herzog's ability to transcend national boundaries of protocol and reserve. Once, when filming in North Korea, he encountered an official who did not want to return Herzog's hard drive for fear it might be used to propagandize against the regime. He offered the man three guarantees. "What are they?" the official asked. Herzog answered, "My honor, my face, and my handshake." To his surprise, he was allowed to keep the hard drive. "And for my part, I never used the material, and never will," Herzog says.

During his rich and storied career, Herzog has directed a wide range of films. He has made twenty full-length fiction movies and seven short fiction films. He has also created thirty-four full-length documentaries, along with eight short ones. In addition to his films, he has directed episodes for two different television series; written many books, including memoirs; and acted in many movies. His most recent acting role was as the Client in the first season of *The Mandalorian*.

CHAPTER THIRTEEN
ANOTHER JOURNEY

In 2000, Juliane's father, Hans Koepcke, falls ill and dies. He never returned to Peru. Perhaps he was too focused on his university work in Germany, or maybe the loss of Maria was so devastating that he couldn't fathom a return to the place where he was so happy.

At forty-six, Juliane inherits Panguana and becomes the lead coordinator for expeditions to the research station. Although her parents' original purchase of the land remains valid, Hans was never able to secure permanent protected status or expand its boundaries. Now the future of Panguana rests solely on Juliane's shoulders. She hopes to fulfill Hans's dream of expansion—but isn't yet sure how to make it happen.

FOLLOW THE WATER

If you're a foreigner in Peru, you're welcomed warmly. You can study in the universities and conduct research in the jungle. You're free to travel, study, work, and marry. However, if you're not a Peruvian citizen, it is very difficult to buy rainforest land for preservation.

Juliane is a native-born citizen of Peru. She returns to Lima eager to expand the size of the station from 460 acres and to establish it as a protected nature and research preserve. But to do this, she will need to test her fortitude in the world of public servants and elected officials.

Bureaucracy is the tangled web of government offices, closed doors, rules, and overworked clerks. To navigate the corridors and meet officials, Juliane trades in her khaki pants and rubber boots for pressed suits and a pair of stylish heels. Her glasses are firmly on her nose, and her hair is carefully brushed and styled.

She calculates each step forward carefully. She is respectful. Her passion shines through. But there are so many doors, and they seem so firmly closed. She moves methodically forward with shoulders squared. She learns how to fill in the paperwork and studies the rules and regulations. The same conversation repeats over and over.

Knock.

Convince.

She must first backtrack and verify the paperwork

ANOTHER JOURNEY

of her parents' original purchase. Moro sets out in the rainforest to talk to old-timers and visit regional offices to confirm the deal that Hans and Maria struck so long ago. He surveys the land and identifies neighboring landowners.

Knock.

Convince.

Doors crack open and people listen. She knows she can find help. New employees, government clerks, and directors in the capital, Lima, arch eyebrows and ask her to fill out forms again. Does she have everything? they ask. Where is the proof? She leans in and smiles. *Let me tell you about Panguana.* She produces the meticulously completed application forms that detail the splendor and value of the forest research station. Frustration discovers her and clings to her heart. She flicks away the idea of failure and moves on.

Knock.

Convince.

Every few days the chorus of support grows. Then a law brings her to a screeching halt.

Lawyers step in when it's revealed that both spouses must be Peruvian citizens and involved in the purchase to buy land in Peru. Juliane's husband is not Peruvian. She remains calm and presses forward. More offices are visited, and eventually an exception is made.

Knock.

Convince.

During Juliane's quest, Peru creates a new Ministry of the Environment, and all the laws and allowances for the rainforest are transferred to the new department. Yes, Juliane can convert Panguana into a nature reserve. The new designation will grant her a forty-year renewable permit for a private conservation area. But she must start from the beginning and redo all the paperwork—every single application.

She picks up her pen and begins.

Knock.

Convince.

This conservation work doesn't just take place in government offices in Lima. Panguana is under constant threat from timber and mineral prospectors. When a valuable hardwood tree or precious metal source is found, unscrupulous business agents try to wheedle it away from local people. They offer much-needed cash for the opportunity to cull the wood. They do this illegally, with no permits or permission from landowners or the government.

Moro and his family are the thin line of protectors. Other neighbors need to be convinced so they too can help protect the forest. Moro and Juliane host officials from the local village to see the work at Panguana. The pair understand that if citizens learn about the resources

ANOTHER JOURNEY

and value of protecting the rainforest, human use and settlement will be measured and managed better.

They go on the radio to discuss the plans for the station. Once the local people recognize the importance of the scientific research, they join the effort to protect Panguana.

Knock.

Convince.

The cost of buying land is prohibitive and Juliane needs help. The owners of a famous German bakery, Hofpfisterei, read one of her articles and offer to help. She feels a wave of gratitude and relief. The end is in sight. She's almost there. Is it possible?

Knock.

Convince.

After years of work, Juliane successfully convinces the Peruvian government to allow Panguana to remain a biological research station and a private conservation area. She expands the area from 460 to 3,954 acres by purchasing land surrounding the station.

Her work continues today.

Panguana is now a permanently protected part of the Amazon rainforest. Hunting, deforestation, mineral extraction, and colonization are forbidden in the area. She successfully defended the research station from the insidious creep of development.

FOLLOW THE WATER

Still one other step remains. Public work. Juliane's personal life is tied to a very public tragedy. She is a private person, and yet, to gain the allies and support she needs to continue to protect Panguana, she knows she must tell her story again, and again.

Public speaking, writing about her struggle in the jungle, and examining moments of the crash are all psychologically challenging. It's exhausting to retell the story and answer the same questions over and over. But for her parents, for Panguana, and for the Amazon rainforest, she will dig deep. She decides to write her autobiography. She revisits every detail of her days in the jungle, the hounding of the press, and her successful efforts to establish Panguana. *When I Fell from the Sky* becomes a bestseller, published in seven languages, and the book tour and interviews garner more support for Panguana and her conservation efforts.

The scientist plunges into celebrity, bravely motivated by a single goal. The vow to make a difference.

EPILOGUE

The long wooden boat pushes through the brown water of the Yuyapichis River. Foamy white wakes lap up the sides. A team of scientists grasp the gunwales and watch the green branches flow by as the wind cools their faces. They occasionally duck to avoid overhanging branches as the boat skirts close to the shore to avoid debris. The raspy calls of the hoatzin mix with the steady *pique-pique* of the outboard motor.

Sitting comfortably near the center of the boat is Juliane. More than fifty years have passed since LANSA Flight 508 crashed in the Amazon. So much time, and yet she can feel the presence of her parents as she sees the jungle slip by in a veil of green. She's not far from the shore that leads to Panguana. There will be no shrill whistle announcing her arrival, and Lobo is long dead, yet there is great anticipation.

The trip to Panguana is easier, since the roads are

FOLLOW THE WATER

better maintained, but the last leg is still by boat and a walk to the station. What was once a family hut and forest kitchen is now a small village. There are guesthouses for visiting scientists, a laboratory, and a "round hut" for sharing and debriefing. A solar-powered pump delivers clean water, and a satellite dish connects the station with the world.

Modern meteorological equipment monitors climate and precipitation changes in Panguana. More than 350 professional scientific papers, reports, and magazine and newspaper articles have been published on the flora and fauna of this protected area. It is the oldest research station in Peru, and studies in Panguana reflect the changes to the land and animals over time. This is a valuable tool in describing and documenting the effects of human habitation and climate change.

All the knowledge and information learned from the Amazon is critical to our survival. Plant life keeps our air clean and stops temperatures around the world from soaring. But there are also medical cures that have their roots in the rainforest. More than 25 percent of prescription drugs used by doctors are sourced from rainforest plants and animals. They are used to treat cancer, pain, diabetes, and many, many other human diseases. Humans have barely scratched the surface of what the Amazon can teach us.

Juliane's work to convince the Peruvian government

EPILOGUE

to designate Panguana as a private reserve was a success. Chain saws and clearing fires have not touched her childhood home. What was once a small research station on the lip of the Amazon forest is now a green universe of more than four square miles of protected land, almost the size of five Central Parks, and still growing.

Areas of the nearby El Sira mountains are also protected. These two regions are part of a scattered jigsaw of national parks, preserves, and sanctuaries that stretch across Amazonia. The parcels create corridors of wildlands. Separated habitats diminish diversity and long-term survival of flora and fauna in protected areas. With wildlife corridors, life can continue to flow through the Amazon, maintaining the health of the planet's green lung. Advocates like Juliane work to grow and join the sanctuaries by buying land and supporting government policy change to protect more of the rainforest from development.

The station also supports several schools that teach students about the rich biodiversity of the rainforest and the threats of deforestation. Juliane understands that through educating young people, we can preserve our future. If we teach the young to know and value the rainforest, they will protect it.

Twenty to thirty students from the local Asháninka elementary school, Pampas Verde, gather in the one-room schoolhouse near the research station before noon on school days. Panguana supports the school with donations of supplies and help with infrastructure. The youngsters visit the reserve to learn about the wildlife and their heritage.

Farther down the river, in the town of Yuyapichis, at the Augusto Durand mixed-grade school, students study an Amazon rainforest curriculum and trek to Panguana for hands-on learning and guided tours through the wonders of the rainforest.

In Lima, students from Waldorf schools occasionally travel to Panguana as part of rotating field programs. Following the Waldorf model, students undertake projects that combine thinking, artistic, and practical skills. Once at Panguana, the student teams train as naturalists, work in the kitchen, and visit farms. They meet and mentor the younger students at Pampas Verde and Augusto Durand. They also meet with the university graduate and undergraduate students and working scientists who come to Panguana every year to study.

Panguana is still an ecological hot spot, and the biodiversity is stunning. Top predators such as jaguars, caimans, and anacondas share the forest with tens of thousands of vertebrate and invertebrate species. International scientists discover new life and observe new behaviors every year.

With all the recognition, dramatic events, press, academic speaking, and a reluctant public persona, Juliane

EPILOGUE

stays steady. She retired as the deputy director of the Bavarian State Collection of Zoology in Germany and now serves full-time as the director of Panguana. She oversees the scientific studies and the growth of the reserve from Germany. She speaks and writes about Panguana and supports the local schools.

In 2019, the government of Peru awarded Juliane the Order of Merit for Distinguished Services, in the Grade of Grand Officer. The honor recognized her academic and scientific career, her renowned research on the flora and fauna of the Peruvian Amazon, and the creation of Panguana. Officials also noted that the work contributed to the improvement of the quality of life of the Asháninka communities living around the reserve.

She visits Panguana every year.

ACKNOWLEDGMENTS

My deepest thanks go to my agent, Stephanie Fretwell-Hill, for her steady belief in this project, and to the team at Little, Brown Books for Young Readers—especially my editor, Samantha Gentry, along with Hannah Weinberg—for their thoughtful guidance and support throughout this journey. And a very special thanks to Cheryl Klein for championing and welcoming the manuscript to its home.

I am especially grateful to the experts who shared their knowledge with such generosity: Ed Pandolfino, Steffen Duncan, John Sterling, and Evan Twomey. For research and editorial insight, my sincere thanks to Karoline Guthrie, Louis Goldie, and Judy Loeven.

To the Castillo Lopez family—thank you for introducing me to the astonishing history and beauty of Peru.

I am indebted to the Johns Hopkins University Science Writing Program for helping me shape and strengthen this work. I am particularly thankful to

ACKNOWLEDGMENTS

Melissa Hendricks, John McQuaid, Kim O'Connell, and the ever-patient and wise Nancy Lord.

Special thanks to the Highlights Foundation and Miranda Paul for their support and inspiration.

To my family—thank you for reading and rereading, for your suggestions, your gentle critiques, and your unwavering encouragement.

And finally, my deep appreciation to Dr. Juliane Koepcke Diller, for the courage to share her story with the world.

BEYOND THE CANOPY
A GUIDE TO PANGUANA AND THE RAINFOREST

Andes Mountains

Juliane and Maria's journey takes them over the center of the Andes Mountains, the longest terrestrial mountain range on Earth. These colossal mountains spread over seven countries. Many of the soaring peaks are ancient volcanoes, and more than four thousand glaciers nestle around the freezing summits. The melting snows of the Andes are the initial source of the Amazon River.

The Andes began to form millions of years ago when the earth's Nazca and South American tectonic plates collided in an ancient seabed, thrusting the mountains twenty thousand feet into the sky. The growth of these mountains reversed the course of the Amazon River, which had initially flowed from the Atlantic to the Pacific Ocean.

The plates are still pressing against each other, so the mountains continue to grow taller, about a third of an inch each year. Because the mountains began life under an ocean, hikers can often find seashells and other marine fossils even at the highest peaks.

Biological Field Stations
Field stations provide hands-on experience in studying ecosystems, wildlife, and environmental changes. They are outdoor laboratories for scientists, students, and anyone fascinated by nature. They also help local communities understand conservation issues and make informed decisions about land use and development.

Many stations, like Panguana, support education programs that train future scientists and conservationists. These stations exist worldwide, from city parks to remote rainforests and floating ocean labs. Some have high-tech equipment, while others consist of basic trails and observation points.

At Panguana, researchers have only begun to uncover the region's biodiversity. So far, they've documented the following:

- Over 500 species of trees
- 380 bird species
- 520 different types of ants—the highest concentration in the world
- An estimated 15,000 species of moths—most still unstudied by science

BEYOND THE CANOPY

Every year, new species are discovered, proving that the Amazon rainforest is one of Earth's last great frontiers.

Caña Brava
Also called wild cane, *caña brava* is a member of the grass family and grows in dense, towering clusters. Though it looks soft and sways in the wind, its rigid stalks are tightly packed, making it almost impossible to move through. This is the massive growth that Juliane worked her way through.

Indigenous communities use *caña brava* for building materials, tools, and medicine. Traditional healers create salves from the plant to treat skin infections and abscesses. Its hollow stems also make it ideal for musical instruments and crafts.

Cloud Forests
Above the lowland rainforest, cool, misty forests cling to the mountains. Clouds rise from the humid jungle, wrapping the slopes in a constant veil of fog. Here, trees twist into crooked, moss-covered shapes, and the soil is thin and nutrient-poor.

Because of their isolation, cloud forests shelter rare and highly specialized species. In the El Sira cloud forest, near Panguana, scientists recently captured footage of these animals:

BEYOND THE CANOPY

- A jaguar, prowling its misty domain
- An Andean bear, South America's only bear species
- The Sira curassow, a critically endangered bird thought to be extinct until it reappeared after thirty years (fewer than 250 Sira curassows are believed to exist, making it one of the rarest birds in the world)

Deciduous and Evergreen Trees
Deciduous trees shed their leaves seasonally, often after a dramatic color change, while evergreen trees keep their leaves year-round. In temperate forests, most evergreens are needle-leaved conifers like pines and firs. In contrast, the Amazon rainforest has no native conifers. Instead, it's home to a rich mix of broad-leaved evergreens and trees that shed their leaves. But unlike in colder climates, rainforest trees don't lose their leaves all at once. Many shed and regrow them gradually, one by one, so the canopy stays green and vibrant all year long.

Dismal Trade
Dismal trade is a historical term that refers to the profession of handling the dead. While every culture has rituals and customs for honoring the deceased, some people have looked down on this work, despite its deep cultural

and emotional importance. In the Amazon, the king vulture is nature's largest undertaker.

Echolocation
Some animals, like bats and dolphins, use echolocation to navigate and hunt. They emit high-frequency sound waves that bounce off objects, helping them map their surroundings.

Bats are experts at echolocation. Their sonar clicks increase in frequency as they home in on prey. Humans can't hear these ultrahigh sounds, but bats also squeak, grunt, and chatter in lower frequencies we can detect.

Ecological Hot Spot
An ecological hot spot is an area with exceptional biodiversity that is threatened by human activity. Even though Panguana is a protected reserve, it remains a hot spot because of the following factors:

- Climate change
- Deforestation
- Amazon basin disruptions

These areas are global conservation priorities, as they contain species found nowhere else on Earth. Scientists race to study them before their ecosystems disappear forever.

BEYOND THE CANOPY

Field Scientists
Field scientists study plants, animals, and ecosystems in the wild. Instead of working in traditional labs, they conduct research outdoors, recording animal behavior, plant growth, and environmental changes.

Some field scientists are famous for their research:

- Jane Goodall (chimpanzees)
- Dian Fossey (mountain gorillas)
- Biruté Galdikas (orangutans)

Their work transformed how we understand primates and conservation.

Flora and Fauna
- Flora = Plant life
- Fauna = Animal life

Originally used by biologists, these words describe the living organisms in a particular region. The term *biota* includes all life-forms, including fungi and microbes.

Schools and Educational Outreach
The Panguana Foundation actively engages in education and outreach initiatives, focusing on schools in neighboring communities, as well as regional and national universities. Through short-term stays and project weeks,

such as "summer schools," students and school classes immerse themselves in the rainforest to develop a deeper awareness of its delicate ecosystem.

These programs help inspire the younger generation and train future decision-makers on the importance of protecting their country's biodiversity.

Beyond education, the foundation also supports social projects in surrounding Asháninka villages. These efforts include the following:

- Improving drinking water supplies
- Assisting with local schools
- Supporting small infrastructure projects

Several Asháninka families live in Pampas Verde, a village three kilometers from Panguana, which is part of the Comunidades Nativas Asháninka Nuevos Unidos Tahuantinsuyo (Asháninka Native Community of Nuevos Unidos Tahuantinsuyo).

Sunbittern

Maria Koepcke, Juliane's mother, admired this small, secretive bird for its extraordinary defense mechanism.

The sunbittern appears brown and easily overlooked, but when threatened, it spreads its wings, revealing two enormous eyelike patterns. To a predator, the little bird suddenly looks like a massive, staring beast, enough to startle a jaguar or other attacker. This dramatic illusion gives the bird precious seconds to escape.

Tectonic Plates
The Earth's crust is divided into shifting slabs called tectonic plates. Their movement over millions of years has shaped continents, oceans, and mountains.

- Colliding plates create volcanoes and mountain ranges (like the Andes).
- Separating plates form deep ocean trenches.
- Shifting plates cause earthquakes.

The Nazca plate and South American plate continue to push the Andes higher each year.

We Are Peruvians
Peru is a country of rich history, diverse cultures, and breathtaking landscapes. The first Peruvians were Indigenous peoples who arrived more than fifteen thousand years ago, migrating from East Asia across the Bering Strait land bridge. Over time, they built advanced civilizations, mastering math, astronomy, medicine, and farming.

The Inca Empire was one of the most powerful societies in South America, ruling in the 1400s and constructing the famous Machu Picchu in the Andes Mountains. However, in the 1500s, Spanish explorers led by Francisco Pizarro arrived, bringing new languages, religions, and traditions—and also war, disease, and hardship for the Indigenous people. Over centuries, immigrants from Spain, Japan, China, and Africa added to Peru's cultural mix, with many Africans arriving through the transatlantic slave trade. Today, over 60 percent of Peruvians are mestizo, meaning they have both Indigenous and immigrant ancestry.

Peru remains a multicultural and multilingual nation. Spanish, Quechua, and Aymara are the official languages, but over ninety Indigenous languages are still spoken, particularly in the Amazon rainforest. Scientists continue to explore ancient ruins, study Amazonian species, and work with Indigenous communities to unlock the secrets of this extraordinary land.

HOW TO BECOME A SCIENTIST

Becoming a scientist is like being a detective for the universe—you get to ask big questions, make discoveries, and explore the unknown. It takes hard work, curiosity, and patience, but if you love learning about the world, there's no better job!

There's no single "right way" to become a scientist, but here are some key steps to help you along the path:

1. **Stay Curious!**
   Scientists are professional question-askers. Poke around, experiment, and figure out how things work. Never stop asking, "Why?" "How?" and "What if?"

2. **Keep an Open Mind**
   Science is about exploration and discovery. Sometimes the answers aren't what you expect—and that's okay! Stay open to new

ideas and be willing to change your mind when new evidence comes along.

3. **Find a Mentor**
   Having a mentor (a teacher, a scientist, or an expert in a field you love) can help you learn faster, ask better questions, and get hands-on experience. Look for science fairs, summer programs, or online communities where scientists share their work.

4. **Get Strong in Science and Math**
   Math is the language of science. Don't worry if it feels tricky at first—even great scientists struggle with it! Ask for help, find a tutor, or work with friends to master difficult topics.

5. **Believe in Yourself**
   Science isn't about being the smartest person in the room—it's about hard work and persistence. If a subject seems tough, don't give up. Keep practicing, ask for help, and keep pushing forward.

6. **Join Science Clubs and Camps**
   Explore different types of science by joining a club, attending summer science camps,

or visiting museums and nature centers. Hands-on experiences can help you discover what excites you most.

7. **Read, Read, Read!**
   Learn about famous scientists and their discoveries. Read books, articles, and websites about different types of science—astronomy, biology, chemistry, engineering, and more. The more you explore, the easier it will be to find your passion.

8. **Become a Certified Naturalist**
   Want to learn real-world science? Look into becoming a certified naturalist! The Alliance of Natural Resource Outreach and Service Programs (ANROSP) offers programs across the country. Find one near you at anrosp.org.

9. **Study in Groups**
   Working with friends can make tough subjects easier (and more fun!). Teaching someone else is one of the best ways to learn, so form study groups and help one another out.

10. **Learn a Foreign Language**
    Science is global, and knowing a second language (like Spanish, French, or Mandarin)

can help you connect with scientists around the world. Many scientific papers and discoveries come from different countries—being bilingual is a huge advantage!

11. **Choose a Science Major That Excites You**
    When it's time for college, pick a major that you're passionate about. Whether it's marine biology, environmental science, physics, or engineering, follow your curiosity!

12. **Get Hands-On Experience**
    Internships and lab assistant jobs give you real-world experience in science. Look for opportunities in college to work in labs, research centers, or conservation programs.

13. **Keep Learning: Graduate School and Research**
    Want to dive deeper? Graduate school allows you to research topics you love and get paid to discover new things. Many scientists get grants or scholarships to continue their studies.

14. **Turn Your Passion into a Career**
    Science isn't just a subject—it's a way of thinking and exploring the world. Whether

HOW TO BECOME A SCIENTIST

you become a researcher, engineer, conservationist, doctor, or astronaut, there's a place for your curiosity in science.

15. Never Stop Exploring!
Science is a lifelong journey. Stay curious, keep learning, and don't be afraid to fail—some of the biggest discoveries in history happened by accident!

FURTHER READING AND VIEWING

Lost in the Amazon: A Battle for Survival in the Heart of the Rainforest, by Tod Olson, Scholastic, 2018

When I Fell from the Sky: The True Story of One Woman's Miraculous Survival, by Juliane Koepcke with Beate Rygiert, translated by Ross Benjamin, TitleTown Publishing, 2011

Wings of Hope, directed by Werner Herzog, made-for-TV movie, 1999, originally aired on the Discovery Channel and now available on Amazon

BIBLIOGRAPHY

ATTO. (n.d.). "Bacteria in the Amazonian Atmosphere." https://attoproject.org/bacteria-in-the-amazonian-atmosphere/.

Avian Report. "Vultures in North, Central, and South America." https://avianreport.com/vultures-in-north-central-and-south-america/.

Barceloux, D. G. "Strychnine." *Disease-a-Month* 58, no. 11 (2012): 624–626. https://doi.org/10.1016/j.disamonth.2012.07.002.

Blue Planet Biomes. "Kapok Tree." Accessed June 18, 2020. https://blueplanetbiomes.org/kapok.php.

Buehler, Jake. "Stingrays in the Amazon Were Stranded There by the Caribbean Sea." *New Scientist*, April 5, 2021. https://newscientist.com/article/2273362-stingrays-in-the-amazon-were-stranded-there-by-the-caribbean-sea/.

Butcher, James, and Molly Doherty. "How Does a Helicopter Fly." *Issuu*, 2016. Accessed June 15, 2020. https://issuu.com/grillustdropbox/docs/how_does_a_helicopter_fly.

Butler, Ryan K., and David P. Finn. "Stress-Induced Analgesia." *Progress in Neurobiology* 88, no. 3 (2009): 184–202.

Clark, Anders. "The Lansa Flight 508 Crash: Juliane Koepcke and 11 Days of Survival." Disciples of

BIBLIOGRAPHY

Flight. https://disciplesofflight.com/the-lansa-flight-508-crash-juliane-koepcke/.
Cornell Lab of Ornithology. "King Vulture." https://ebird.org/species/kinvul1.
Grit Podcast. "Episode 3 Without Wings." December 22, 2016. https://archive.org/details/Episode3WithoutWings.
Hartl, Judith. "Amazon: Abundant Rainforests, Useless Soils." DW. August 23, 2019. https://dw.com/en/the-amazon-nutrient-rich-rainforests-on-useless-soils/a-50139632.
Henze, Gunnar. Paradies Panguana. Bild Der Wissenschaft Online—Heftarchiv. Archived September 23, 2015. https://web.archive.org/web/20150923185338/http:/www.bild-der-wissenschaft.de/bdw/bdwlive/heftarchiv/index2.php?object_id=32705136.
"Incredible Fall of Juliane Koepcke, The." Natura Pop. Accessed June 18, 2020. https://www.naturapop.com/articles-a-window-to-natural-philosophy/the-incredible-fall-of-juliane-koepcke.
Journal, The. "This Woman Was the Sole Survivor of a Flight Obliterated by a Thunderstorm." September 5, 2015. https://www.thejournal.ie/survivor-plane-crash-2302815-Sep2015/.
Koepcke, Juliane. "How I Survived a Plane Crash." *BBC News*, March 24, 2012. https://bbc.com/news/magazine-17476615.
Koepcke, Juliane. *Ökologische Studien an einer Fledermaus-Artengemeinschaft im tropischen Regenwald von Peru*, 1987.
Koepcke, Juliane. *When I Fell From the Sky: The True Story of One Woman's Miraculous Survival*. TitleTown Publishing, LLC, 2011. Kindle.
Lentink, D., W. B. Dickson, J. L. van Leeuwen, and M. H. Dickinson. "Leading-Edge Vortices Elevate Lift of Autorotating Plant Seeds." *Science* 324, no. 5933 (June 12, 2009): 1438–40. https://doi.org/10.1126/science.1174196.

BIBLIOGRAPHY

Lentink, David. "Maple Seeds and Animals Exploit the Same Trick to Fly." California Institute of Technology, June 11, 2009. https://caltech.edu/about/news/maple-seeds-and-animals-exploit-same-trick-fly-1540.

Lieberson, Alan D. "How Long Can a Person Survive Without Food?" *Scientific American*, November 8, 2004. https://scientificamerican.com/article/how-long-can-a-person-survive-without-food/.

Littlewood, Tom. "The Woman Who Fell to Earth." *Vice*, September 2, 2010. https://vice.com/en_us/article/8gmgmz/the-woman-who-fell-to-earth-508-v17n9.

Mehanna, Hisham M., Jamil Moledina, and Jane Travis. "Refeeding Syndrome: What It Is, and How to Prevent and Treat It." *BMJ* 336, no. 7659 (June 26, 2008): 1495–98. https://doi.org/10.1136/bmj.a301.

Met Office. "Cumulonimbus Clouds." https://weather.metoffice.gov.uk/learn-about/weather/types-of-weather/clouds/low-level-clouds/cumulonimbus.

Mourtzi, Niki, Amalia Sertedaki, and Evangelia Charmandari. "Glucocorticoid Signaling and Epigenetic Alterations in Stress-Related Disorders." *International Journal of Molecular Sciences* 22, no. 11 (2021). https://doi.org/10.3390/ijms22115964.

Museo de Historia Natural. "Exposición temporal: Explorando la biodiversidad de Panguana." https://museohn.unmsm.edu.pe/panguana.html.

National Center for Biotechnology Information. "In Brief: How Does Skin Work?" Updated April 5, 2022. https://ncbi.nlm.nih.gov/books/NBK279255/.

Natural History Museum. "The Schmidt Sting Pain Index." https://www.nhm.ac.uk/discover/schmidt-pain-index-insect-stings.html.

BIBLIOGRAPHY

NHS. "Causes – Post-Traumatic Stress Disorder." Reviewed May 13, 2022. https://nhs.uk/mental-health/conditions/post-traumatic-stress-disorder-ptsd/causes/.

O'Meara, Brendan, host. The Creative Nonfiction Podcast. "Episode 132: Laura Hillenbrand on Research Workarounds, Reading Aloud, and Campfire Storytelling." Accessed June 15, 2020. https://brendanomeara.com/hillenbrand132/.

"Panguana." Panguana Siftung. Accessed June 18, 2020. https://panguana.de/?lang=en/.

Papathanasiou, Katerina. "Juliane Koepcke: The Sole Survivor of the LANSA Flight 508." *The Vale Magazine*, April 8, 2020. https://thevalemagazine.com/2020/04/08/juliane-koepcke-survivor-plane-crash/.

Peru Aves. "King Vulture (*Sarcoramphus papa*)." https://peruaves.org/cathartidae/king-vulture-sarcoramphus-papa/.

Peru Aves. "Tawny-Crowned Greenlet (*Tunchiornis ochraceiceps*)." https://peruaves.org/vireonidae/tawny-crowned-greenlet-hylophilus-ochraceiceps/.

Peruvian Government. "Condecoran a Juliane Koepcke por su labor científica y académica en la Amazonía peruana." June 18, 2020. https://www.gob.pe/institucion/rree/noticias/27182-condecoran-a-juliane-koepcke-por-su-labor-cientifica-y-academica-en-la-amazonia-peruana.

Pleitgen, Frederik. "Survivor Still Haunted by 1971 Air Crash." CNN. July 2, 2009. https://web.archive.org/web/20180225140559/http:/www.cnn.com/2009/WORLD/europe/07/02/germany.aircrash.survivor/index.html.

Romero, Andrea, Jessica Montaño, Anthony Soto Cedeño, and Gonçal Oliveros Layola. "First Report of Bullet Ants (*Paraponera clavata*) Sequestering Vertebrate Carrion." *Food Webs* 24 (September 2020). https://doi.org/10.1016/j.fooweb.2020.e00151.

BIBLIOGRAPHY

Scott. "A 17 Year Old Girl Survived a 2 Mile Fall Without a Parachute, Then Trekked Alone 10 Days Through the Peruvian Rainforest." *Today I Found Out* (blog). April 11, 2012. https://todayifoundout.com/index.php/2012/04/a-17-year-old-girl-survived-a-2-mile-fall-without-a-parachute-then-trekked-alone-10-days-through-the-peruvian-rainforest/.

Smithsonian's National Zoo and Conservation Biology Institute. "Freshwater Stingray." https://nationalzoo.si.edu/animals/freshwater-stingray.

U.S. Department of the Interior. "13 Awesome Facts About Bats." October 24, 2024. https://doi.gov/blog/13-facts-about-bats.

Various. "#koepcke Instagram Posts (Photos and Videos)" Picuki.com. Accessed June 18, 2020. https://picuki.com/tag/koepcke.

Vuilleumier, Francois. "Hans-Wilhelm Koepcke." *Ornitologia Neotropical* 13, no. 2 (2002): 215–18.

Weather Spark. "Climate and Average Weather Year Round in Tournavista, Peru." https://weatherspark.com/y/23294/Average-Weather-in-Tournavista-Peru-Year-Round.

Weitekamp, Margaret, and Dorothy Cochrane. "Geraldyn 'Jerrie' Cobb: Pioneering Woman Aviator." National Air and Space Museum. April 18, 2019. https://airandspace.si.edu/stories/editorial/remembering-geraldyn-jerrie-cobb-pioneering-woman-aviator.

Williams, Sally. "Sole Survivor: The Woman Who Fell to Earth." *The Telegraph*, March 22, 2012. https://telegraph.co.uk/culture/books/authorinterviews/9143701/Sole-survivor-the-woman-who-fell-to-earth.html.

Zoologische Staatssammlung München. "Panguana." Accessed June 18, 2020. https://zsm.snsb.de/panguana/.

Jolanne Tierney

ELLEN COCHRANE

is a public school teacher, writer, and neighborhood volunteer. When she's not writing, she can be found on her bike or paddling her kayak. *Follow the Water* is Ellen's authorial debut. She invites you to visit her at ellencochrane.com.

CELEBRATING 100 YEARS OF PUBLISHING

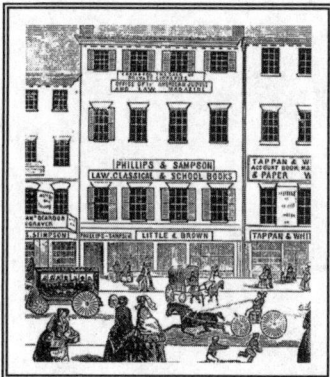

Dear Reader,

You may have noticed the words "Little, Brown and Company" on the title page of this book and wondered what they mean. Well, Charles C. Little and James Brown were the founders of this publishing house, and the "and Company" is all the editors, designers, marketers, publicists, salespeople, and more who help produce each book and bring it to readers like you. Little, Brown was founded in Boston, Massachusetts, in 1837, and some of its early publications included *The Writings of George Washington* and *The Works of Benjamin Franklin*. The catalog grew to feature works by Emily Dickinson and Louisa May Alcott, among many other notable authors. In 1926, recognizing that the literature we read when we are young has a deep and lasting influence and requires expert curation, the company appointed an editor to lead a dedicated children's department.

In 2026, Little, Brown Books for Young Readers celebrates one hundred years of excellence in publishing. Today, we are a division of Hachette Livre, the third-largest publisher in the world, and we are based in New York City. Our staff has grown from a team of two to more than one hundred people. And with the changes in technology, our books are read by more readers, in more ways, and in more countries than ever before. However, one thing has not changed: our commitment to providing a supportive home for all creators and superb stories for all readers. Thank you for being one of them.

Megan Tingley
Megan Tingley
President and Publisher

LITTLE, BROWN AND COMPANY
BOOKS FOR YOUNG READERS

To learn more about Little, Brown's history, authors, and books, please visit LBYR.com.